LOVE'S GOT EVERYTHING TO DO WITH IT

ROSEMARIE KARLEBACH

Go after a life of love as if your life depended on it — because it does.
1 Corinthians 14:1 *The Message*

Cover and Jacket Design: Jeffrey Mobley Design Tulsa, OK

HENSLEY
PUBLISHING

Introduction

What's love got to do with it? That's probably one of the most relevant questions asked lately. Certainly, it deserves an answer. According to the lyrics Tina Turner sings, it's a "second-hand emotion." Yet a lot of people are pursuing love.

But what is love, really? An emotion? A myth fabricated by Hollywood? The stuff of which only dreams are made? Can love really exist in this age of skyrocketing statistics of domestic violence and divorce?

I have excellent news for you, my friend. Despite indications to the contrary, love is still alive and well and flourishing on planet earth! But not in the form most people imagine.

On the following pages, you'll have an opportunity to take a look at the many facets of true love. Together we'll look at not only its beginning, but also its future. It will be an exciting adventure as we gain new insight into the most beautiful endowment ever bequeathed by a generous Father to His beloved child — you!

So, the question is, "What's love got to do with it?"

My prayer is that by the end of our journey together you'll be able to see what wonderful things Love has in store for you, and resoundingly respond — "Everything!"

Dedication

This book is lovingly dedicated to all of my family, both natural and spiritual: my Lord and Savior, Jesus Christ, who first loved me; my husband Paul and daughters, Jasmine and Ariel, whose love gave me the impetus from which to write this book; my mother, Geri, sisters, Phyllis, Nancy, Billie; their husbands, Keith and Tim; Paul's parents, Dorrit and Frank, all of whom have loved me over the years in spite of my shortcomings; my dearest friends, Sherry, Connie, Nancy and Sheri, who have consistently seen and brought out the very best in me — thank you for your gifts of unconditional love — and, of course, my editor, Terri, and publisher, Neal, without whose love and support this book would never have been written in the first place.

Contents

What Is Love?

~∾~

God is Love.
1 John 4:16

~∾~

What usually comes to your mind when you think of love? A beautiful story? Romantic music? Or, do you think of love as only an emotion or feeling? Is love something you've experienced to your heart's satisfaction, or is it at best, something illusive, the stuff of which only your sweetest dreams are made? Whatever the case may be, many of us find ourselves asking the same question: Can I really experience true love, or is it reserved for only a handful of fortunate few?

We see many counterfeits these days, relationships that advertise themselves as love, only to end up as heartache and disaster. Perhaps, as another old song has said, we're "looking for love in all the wrong places."

The pursuit of love is noble; in fact, it's God-inspired. Before we can actually experience a fulfilling love, however, whether with a spouse or friend, we have to understand what love is and what its roots and purpose are. Without that knowledge, we're left to fend for ourselves, fingers crossed behind our backs, hoping it will work out. To gain a better understanding of the subject, then, our best bet would be to go back to love's beginning.

Before Shakespeare ever penned his beloved classic, "Romeo and Juliet," before the Greeks were inspired to sculpt their lovely Venus; even before Adam and Eve ever set one foot in the garden, there was love, and that love began in the very heart of God. We humans try to deny this point, as if we somehow manufactured it, but in 1 John 4:16, the Bible says *God is love*. God — not Shakespeare, not Hollywood — is the beginning and source of love. His love existed before the foundation of the world (John 17:24). He is the One from Whom love emanates. Without Him, love does not exist.

Since God is the Source of love, it's only logical to go to Him to gain greater insight into the subject. Because His very nature is love, He has provided us with a handbook to learn about the subject. That handbook is His Word to us, the Bible. For our purposes, then, that's just the place we'll start, with the Bible, God's inspired Word to you. As we look at it together, you will discover not only that God is love, but also just how very much He loves you, personally. Keep that in mind as we look at the many facets of love.

~ Life Application ~

1. Read 1 John 4:16 again. What does it say God is? What does that mean to you? Write down your thoughts.

   _____

   _____

   _____

   _____

2. Look up Ephesians 1:4. According to this scripture, how long have God and His love existed?

   _____

   _____

   _____

   _____

3. According to 1 John 4:19, why are we able to love God?

   _____

   _____

   _____

   _____

4. Read 1 Thessalonians 4:9. Who teaches love? Why would that be?

   _____

   _____

   _____

   _____

~ Journal ~

Write what you think and how you feel when you hear the words, "God loves you."

_____

_____

_____

_____

_____

_____

_____

_____

_____

_____

_____

_____

_____

_____

_____

_____

_____

_____

_____

_____

_____

_____

Love Is A Person

~≈~

*God created man in His own image, in the image
and likeness of God He created him; male and
female He created them.*

Genesis 1:27

~≈~

We've already seen that God is love, but did you know
that Genesis 1:26-27 tells us we are just like God? Each of
us is born with a personality, so it stands to reason that God
has a personality, too. He created us just like Himself, for
the purpose of love.

Knowing God is a person makes it easier for us to
love Him. It's hard to love a "flow" or a "warm fuzzy
feeling," but it's not hard to love another person, especially
One as wonderful and loving as God.

God, just like any person, wants those He loves to
love Him in return. That is, in essence, why He created
you in the first place. Although He does have something
for you to do in life, the most important thing He designed
you for is to fellowship with Him.

God wants you to love Him as much as He loves you.
Look what He says about the person who loves Him.
*Because he has set his love upon Me, therefore will I deliver
him; I will set him on high, because he knows and
understands My name [has a personal knowledge of My*

mercy, love, and kindness — trusts and relies on Me, knowing I will never forsake him, no, never]. He shall call upon Me, and I will answer him; I will be with him in trouble, I will deliver him and honor him. With long life will I satisfy him and show him My salvation (Psalm 91:14-16). That's quite a statement. This is how much God will do for the person who loves Him.

God wants to have fellowship with you. Just as you like to be with your loved ones, He desires your companionship. He would like nothing better than for you to spend time sitting with Him, talking to Him, experiencing His presence. In Psalm 16:11, King David said of God, *"You will show me the path of life; in Your presence is fullness of joy."* David was considered a man after God's own heart; he must have known something about having fellowship with God.

In Song of Solomon 2:14, the shepherd, who represents God, says to you, *"O My dove, [while you are here] in the seclusion of the clefts in the solid rock, in the sheltered and secret place of the cliff, let me see your face, let me hear your voice; for your voice is sweet and your face is lovely."* This is how God feels about you. He wants to see your face. He wants to hear your sweet voice. This is His desire, more than anything else. So, spend time with Him. Love Him.

Treat Him as you would treat any other person you deeply love. Make Him a priority in your life. Just as King David experienced, let God show you the path of life, so you can have fullness of joy in fellowship with Him.

～ Life Application ～

1. What does Genesis 1:26-27 mean when it says you were made in God's image and likeness? Does it just mean you look like God? Explain.

    _____

    _____

    _____

2. Why is it important to know love is a person, not just a feeling?

    _____

    _____

    _____

3. Why did God make you in His image and likeness?

    _____

    _____

    _____

4. Does God desire your fellowship? Why?

    _____

    _____

    _____

5. Read Psalm 91:14-16 What does God promise to do for the person who loves Him?

    _____

    _____

~ Journal ~

Read Song of Solomon 2:14 again. Why does God want to hear your voice and see your face? Did you know He felt that way about you?

_____

_____

_____

_____

_____

_____

_____

_____

_____

_____

_____

_____

_____

_____

_____

_____

_____

_____

_____

_____

Love Has A Nature

~∾~

Love endures long and is patient and kind; love never is envious nor boils over with jealousy, is not boastful or vainglorious, does not display itself haughtily. It is not conceited (arrogant and inflated with pride); it is not rude (unmannerly) and does not act unbecomingly. Love (God's love in us) does not insist on its own rights or its own way, for it is not self-seeking; it is not touchy or fretful or resentful; it takes no account of the evil done to it [it pays no attention to a suffered wrong]. It does not rejoice at injustice and unrighteousness, but rejoices when right and truth prevail. Love bears up under anything and everything that comes, is ever ready to believe the best of every person, its hopes are fadeless under all circumstances, and it endures everything [without weakening]. Love never fails [never fades out or becomes obsolete or comes to an end].

1 Corinthians 13:4-8

~∾~

We often measure our relationship with God by the successes or failures we've had in relationships with others. We somehow blame God for their failures — even when we haven't bothered to involve Him in those relationships in the first place. Proverbs 14:12 says *there is a way which seems right to a man and appears straight before him, but at the end of it is the way of death*. We sometimes think we're doing the right thing getting involved in a relationship we haven't consulted God about; but it's actually only going to end up in disaster.

God's love, on the other hand, cannot be measured by human standards. In Isaiah 55:8 God says, *"My thoughts are not your thoughts, neither are your ways My ways…For as the heavens are higher than the earth, so are My ways higher than your ways and My thoughts than your thoughts."* What possible difference can it make to us that God's ways are higher than ours? This: We cannot judge God's love by the experiences we've had with others. For instance: People get divorced every day. Does that necessarily mean it's God's will for them? Of course not; but some of us have been tempted to think it does.

Do you often think that when something happens to you it must be God's plan for you? The exact opposite may actually be true. Keep in mind, God has a good plan for you.

First Corinthians 13:8 shows us exactly what God's love is like. It's not at all like the changeable human love you may have experienced. It's a supernatural love, a higher, superior love. In fact, if you've experienced love at all the way 1 Corinthians 13:8 describes it, you've probably met someone who knows God well.

You can only experience God's kind of love through a personal relationship with Him. This is actually His desire, and it has been through the ages. He wants to know and love you, and to be known and loved by you in return. Do you desire this kind of love? If so, the first thing to do is to open your heart to Him so you can experience His supernatural love for yourself.

~ Life Application ~

1. Look at 1 Corinthians 13:4-8 and write down some of the characteristics of God's love.

   _____

   _____

   _____

2. Could you have a successful relationship with someone who demonstrated love for you in this way? Why?

   _____

   _____

   _____

3. Do you think it would make it easier to love others if you had this kind of love in your heart? Why?

   _____

   _____

   _____

4. What does "love bears up under anything" mean to you? Were you aware that this is a characteristic of God's love, or did you think something else was the case?

   _____

   _____

   _____

   _____

~ Journal ~

Take some time to meditate on (think about) 1 Corinthians 13:4-8, taking each characteristic and visualizing yourself receiving and operating in it. How would this kind of love in your heart affect your relationships? What difference could it make in your life?

_____

_____

_____

_____

_____

_____

_____

_____

_____

_____

_____

_____

_____

_____

_____

_____

_____

_____

Love Is A Process

~≈~

In this [union and communion with Him] love is
brought to completion and attains perfection with
us....We love Him, because He first loved us.
1 John 4:17, 19

~≈~

The Bible tells us that God is the Source of Love, and that without Him there can be no love. This is the real reason for unsuccessful relationships. No matter how hard you may try to make a relationship work, you cannot truly love another if you aren't convinced of God's love for you. And you can't have His love in your heart if you have no close, personal relationship with Him. God wants to be involved in your relationships. He wants you to experience love, not only from Him, but from others as well. But how do you include God in your relationships?

We've already established that God is love and that He loves you. According to Hebrews 11:6, the next move is yours: *Whoever would come near to God must [necessarily] believe that God exists and that He is the rewarder of those who earnestly and diligently seek Him [out].* God wants you to believe that He **is**. If you've ever seen the love of a mother for a newborn baby, or experienced love of any sort, then you know God exists, because He is love. The next step is to seek Him — and you're doing just that as you read these pages. His promise to you is that He will reward you as you seek Him out. What will He reward you with? With love, of course, from both Himself and others. Your job is just to seek and trust Him.

James 4:8 says if you *come close to God…He will come close to you.* That's the start in a relationship with God. All it takes is the desire to know more about God, and His love. Then, as 1 John 4:19 says: *We love Him, because He first loved us.* You see, you can't even begin to love without receiving God's love first; and you will come to love Him more as you understand His love more fully. Keep in mind, learning to love is an ongoing process. There are no human experts because there's always more to learn. The key is your desire to experience God's love more fully.

Ephesians 3:19 shows us God's will concerning love: *[That you may really come] to know [practically, through experience for yourselves] the love of Christ…that you may be filled [through all your being] unto all the fullness of God.* As your understanding of God's love for you grows, you will begin fulfilling Leviticus 19:18: *You shall love your neighbor as yourself.* You can then begin to love others in a greater measure than ever before because you will be fully convinced of and overflowing with God's wonderful, abundant love.

~ Life Application ~

1. According to 1 John 4:19, with whom does the love process start?

   _____

   _____

   _____

   _____

2. Is it important for you to know how much God loves you in order for you to love others?

   _____

   _____

   _____

   _____

3. Read Hebrews 11:6. What two things must you believe to begin the process of love?

   _____

   _____

   _____

   _____

4. How do you think God rewards you?

   _____

   _____

   _____

   _____

~ Journal ~

Ephesians 3:19 explains the process of love. What are some ways you can experience God's love more fully? Write down your thoughts.

_____

_____

_____

_____

_____

_____

_____

_____

_____

_____

_____

_____

_____

_____

_____

_____

_____

_____

_____

_____

Love Is Good

~≈~

Every good gift and every perfect (free, large, full) gift is from above; it comes down from the Father of all [that gives] light, in [the shining of] Whom there can be no variation [rising or setting] or shadow cast by His turning [as in an eclipse].

James 1:17

~≈~

Isn't it amazing how, despite the proliferation of TV programming, you can't find many examples of good old-fashioned loving relationships anymore. Instead, we're bombarded with bizarre relationships which go from bad to disastrous, where the partners treat each other worse than enemies, while saying they're "in love." Are they really? The truth is, they're not, because love, like God, is good and produces good fruit.

Galatians 5:22 tells us what good fruit God's love, through His Holy Spirit, produces in our lives: *The fruit of the [Holy] Spirit [the work which His presence within accomplishes] is love, joy (gladness), peace, patience (an even temper, forbearance), kindness, goodness (benevolence), faithfulness, gentleness (meekness, humility), self-control (self-restraint, continence).* These fruit are all "good and perfect" gifts from God. With them, you can have a lasting relationship. With them, everything works out for good.

God wants only the best for our lives. He wants us to be happy and prosperous and productive. Everything He does for us and gives to us is toward that end. The same is true with love, probably God's greatest gift to mankind. God created us first to be loved by Him, to love Him in return, and then to have loving relationships with others here on earth.

Many of us, however, are confused about love. We associate it with unpleasant things. We don't realize that God's love is a good love. But without God's love active in our hearts and lives, our relationships are left to themselves and doomed to fail. Galatians 5:19-21 gives us an idea of how our human nature acts without God. *Now the doings (practices) of the flesh are clear (obvious): they are immorality, impurity, indecency, idolatry, sorcery, enmity, strife, jealousy, anger (ill temper), selfishness, divisions (dissensions), party spirit (factions, sects with peculiar opinions, heresies), envy, drunkenness, carousing, and the like.* Don't these characteristics resemble the behavior on daytime soap operas and talk shows? Without a doubt.

It is vitally important that we understand the difference between this kind of godless behavior and God's good love. One kind of behavior brings sorrow and death, of either a spiritual or physical nature; the other brings joy and life.

Psalm 23:6 says: *Only goodness, mercy and unfailing love shall follow me all the days of my life.* This is God's wonderful plan for you — not heartache, strife, fighting or a broken heart. He would never involve you in a relationship in which your heart would be broken, but if you do experience one, He's so good He'll even mend it for you!

Philippians 1:6 says: *He Who began a good work in you will continue until the day of Jesus Christ [right up to the time of His return], developing [that good work] and perfecting and bringing it to full completion in you.* God has a good work for you to do. If you'll cooperate with Him, He will develop and bring it to completion. So, the next time you're tempted to get involved in a relationship that is less than good, remember, it's not from God, because God's gifts are always good. All the time.

~ Life Application ~

1. According to James 1:17, what kind of gifts does the Father give? Give some examples which you have received in your life.

    _____

    _____

    _____

    _____

2. Read Galatians 5:16-25. List the works of the flesh (godless behavior). Is this what you want in a relationship?

    _____

    _____

    _____

    _____

3. List the fruit of the Spirit according to Galatians 5:22. Would you like to experience this in a relationship?

    _____

    _____

    _____

    _____

4. Read Philippians 1:6 again. Does God do good or bad works?

    _____

~ Journal ~

Consider some of the relationships you've experienced in your life. Were they controlled by the Holy Spirit? Do you think some of them might have been different if they had been controlled by the Spirit? What are some obvious signs that will help you tell the difference in the future?

_____

_____

_____

_____

_____

_____

_____

_____

_____

_____

_____

_____

_____

_____

_____

_____

_____

_____

_____

Love Never Changes

~≈~

The Lord appeared from of old to me…saying, Yes, I have loved you with an everlasting love; therefore with loving-kindness have I drawn you and continued My faithfulness to you.

Jeremiah 31:3

~≈~

Most relationships can be very fickle. One day everything is just peachy-keen, and the next day all hell breaks loose. That's why we see so many divorces nowadays. The "love" is based on ideal circumstances; as they vanish, so does love. But aren't we looking for someone to love us no matter what? There's no way we can be on our best behavior all the time, and it's unpleasant to think that a little slip-up could be the death-knell of a relationship.

The Bible says in Hebrews 13:8: *Jesus Christ (the Messiah) is [always] the same, yesterday, today, [yes] and forever (to the ages).* God never changes in the way He thinks or feels toward you. He doesn't love you only when you're good and abandon you when you're bad. God's love is unconditional. Psalm 100:5 says: *The Lord is good; His mercy and loving-kindness are everlasting, His faithfulness and truth endure to all generations.* God's mercy and loving-kindness toward you are everlasting. That means that along your journey through life, you can go to Him — in fact He wants you to go to Him — if you blow it. He's willing to forgive. First Corinthians 13:7 says of God's love: *Its hopes are fadeless under all circumstances, and it endures everything [without weakening].* God's love toward you doesn't stop. It keeps right on coming, no matter what. God's in this with you for the long-haul. He's not going to take you halfway along your journey and then say to you, "Well, you really blew it this time. You're on your own. I'm outta here!" That's not His style.

In Matthew 28:20, Jesus said, *"Behold, I am with you all the days (perpetually, uniformly, and on every occasion), to the [very] close and consummation of the age."* Here we see all the aspects of the fact that God's love never changes. First, He loves you now and will love you forever. Second, His love toward you never changes; it's not hot one day and cold the next, it's constant; uniform. Third, no matter what kind of situation you're in, He still loves you, even in the midst of that situation. Whether you're moving smoothly along the path of life or you've hit a snag, He's still there for you. Now, that's an awfully good deal; do you know any other friend you can count on the way you can count on God? Isn't it nice to know that His love toward you will never change?

～ Life Application ～

1. Read Hebrews 13:8 again. What does it mean to you that Jesus is the same, yesterday, today and forever?

    _____

    _____

    _____

    _____

2. How does that thought comfort you?

    _____

    _____

    _____

    _____

3. Read Matthew 28:20 again. What does it mean that Jesus is with you: Perpetually? Uniformly? On every occasion?

    _____

    _____

    _____

    _____

4. What does God mean when He says He loves you with an everlasting love? How does that make you feel?

    _____

    _____

    _____

~ Journal ~

Malachi 3:6 says: *I am the Lord, I do not change*. Take some time to really meditate upon this scripture. Can you see how knowing that God's love toward you never changes will add stability to your life? Write down your thoughts.

_____

_____

_____

_____

_____

_____

_____

_____

_____

_____

_____

_____

_____

_____

_____

_____

_____

_____

_____

Love Is A Response

~⁓~

*You must love the Lord your God with all your heart
and with all your soul and with all your strength and
with all your mind.*

Luke 10:27

~⁓~

Scripture tells us to love God with our heart, soul, mind and strength. But how do you do that exactly? Psalm 119:5 gives us a clue: *Oh, that my ways were directed and established to observe Your statutes [hearing, receiving, loving, and obeying them]!* We are told to love His Word with our hearts; to receive His Word with our souls; to hear His Word with our minds; and to obey with our strength, (our bodies). This is a pretty concise definition of how to love God.

Keep in mind that love is a process. You learn how to love, little by little, step by step. It may not come naturally to you; perhaps you've been hurt in the past through some relationship. That's why God wants to start with your heart. You love God with your heart by trusting Him with your life; by opening up your heart to Him and letting Him have access to it. You allow yourself to be vulnerable to Him, so He can put together the broken pieces if need be. Proverbs 3:5 tells you to *lean on, trust in, and be confident in the Lord with all your heart.* After you've opened up to

Him and He's healed you, you'll be confident of His Word.

It also says to love God with all your mind...*and do not rely on your own insight or understanding*. As you study God's manual — the Bible — you'll begin to see how He thinks, and your thoughts will begin to line up with His will. A whole new, wonderful way of thinking will open up to you. As you present your mind to Him, allow Him to change it, just like your heart.

You love God with your soul by sharing and offering Him your emotions and feelings. As you do this, you become the master of your emotions instead of the slave. Proverbs 3:6 says it well: *In all your ways know, recognize, and acknowledge Him, and He will direct and make straight and plain your paths*. God is your partner; He'll guide you on your journey.

Finally, you love God with your strength by obeying Him. John 14:15 says it best: *If you [really] love Me, you will keep (obey) My commands*. When all is said and done, if you're doing what God says, He can see by your actions that you truly love Him.

So, God is asking you to love Him with every part of your being. Completely. Wholeheartedly. Earnestly. Honestly. Sincerely. As you do this, you'll see His love manifested to you in greater ways. God has always loved you, but as you respond to Him in wholehearted love, you'll begin to see Him much more actively and obviously involved in your day-to-day affairs.

～ Life Application ～

What does it mean to you to love the Lord with your whole heart?

_____

_____

_____

_____

_____

Your whole soul?

_____

_____

_____

_____

Your whole mind?

_____

_____

_____

Your whole strength?

_____

_____

_____

~ Journal ~

Read Luke 10:27 again. Are there any areas of your life that you haven't surrendered to God in love? Have you been loving Him with your whole heart, soul, mind and strength? If not, how can you in the future?

_____

_____

_____

_____

_____

_____

_____

_____

_____

_____

_____

_____

_____

_____

_____

_____

_____

_____

Love Is A Progression

~≈~

You must love the Lord your God…and your neighbor as yourself.

Luke 10:27

~≈~

Love is a progression which begins with God and moves through us to others. Because God is a spirit, He can love others through us. We, then, are His ambassadors, His heart and hands extended to the world, as we share His love. Matthew 22:39 tells us: *You shall love your neighbor as [you do] yourself.* It isn't as hard as it sounds; loving others will become a natural by-product of your relationship with God.

Here's where the progression takes on a whole new, wonderful twist. In Matthew 10:42, Jesus says, *"Whoever gives to one of these…because he is My disciple, surely I declare to you, he shall not lose his reward."* And in Matthew 25:40, He says, *"The King will reply to them, Truly I tell you, in so far as you did it for one of the least [in the estimation of men] of these My brethren, you did it for Me."* Here God is saying that when you love others, you are actually loving Him. That's pretty amazing. Not only do you love God by loving Him directly, but you also love Him by loving others. Look at His promise to you in Proverbs 19:17: *He who has pity on the poor lends to the Lord, and that which he has given He will repay to him.* God is not only pleased when you love others, He also promises you a reward for doing so.

Luke 6:38 says this about giving to others: *Give, and [gifts] will be given to you; good measure, pressed down, shaken together, and running over, will they pour into [the pouch formed by] the bosom [of your robe and used as a bag].* You see, when you give to others, you receive back many times what you've given away. Look also at Ephesians 3:20, which tells us about what God returns to us: *Now to Him Who, by (in consequence of) the [action of His] power that is at work within us, is able to [carry out His purpose and] do superabundantly, far over and above all that we [dare] ask or think [infinitely beyond our highest prayers, desires, thoughts, hopes, or dreams].* You see, God is a God of life and of increase. When He gives back to you, He gives you interest on what you've loaned Him.

According to Proverbs 28:20, *a faithful man shall abound with blessings.* As you love God by loving others, God will reward you for your faithfulness. As you are blessed, you, in turn, will be instrumental in others being drawn to come to know and love God, and the progression of love will continue.

~ Life Application ~

1. Love's progression has an order. Write it down.

   _____

   _____

   _____

   _____

2. Read Matthew 22:37-39 and Luke 10:27. What similar thoughts do these scriptures express? What is the greatest commandment? Why does God consider it so?

   _____

   _____

   _____

   _____

3. Why can't you truly love others if you don't know God's love?

   _____

   _____

   _____

4. Matthew 10:42 speaks of a reward. Describe how you think the Lord might reward you for loving others.

   _____

   _____

   _____

   _____

~ Journal ~

Read Ephesians 3:17-20. According to this, if you become fully aware of and operate in God's love, what is God able to do for you? Take time and really meditate on these scriptures before you answer.

_____

_____

_____

_____

_____

_____

_____

_____

_____

_____

_____

_____

_____

_____

_____

_____

_____

Love Is A Quest

~∾~

Eagerly pursue and seek to acquire [this] love [make it your aim, your great quest].

1 Corinthians 14:1

~∾~

Most of us truly want love in our lives. This is as it should be. God put that desire in our hearts. But God wants us to pursue His love before we pursue any other. His love brings wholeness and joy. This is the love He encourages us to seek, not the kind of love which only leaves brokenness and sorrow in its wake.

First Corinthians 13:5 tells us love is not "self-seeking." This means that when we operate in God's love, we don't concern ourselves with taking care of number one (ourselves), because we know that when we operate like our loving Heavenly Father, we will automatically receive a return on that love. Galatians 6:7, 9 tell us: *whatever a man sows, that and that only he will reap…let us not lose heart and grow weary and faint in acting nobly and doing right, for in due time and at the appointed season we shall reap, if we do not loosen and relax our courage and faint.* God wants us to give our love away, to share it with others. When we start first with a relationship with Him, we are then able to love others. In a sense, then, when you love God first and then love others before yourself, it is really the most "selfish" thing you can do — because God Himself, through His Word, guarantees you a return on the love you give away.

We mustn't be naive enough to think, however, that pursuing love guarantees us freedom from trouble. As Galatians 6:9 tells us, if we don't grow weary, and weak, halfhearted or fearful in doing what's right — if we don't give up on pursuing love — at the appointed time we will reap. Eventually, loving God and others will bring us big dividends — and that's one offer we'd be foolish to refuse.

In Acts 20:35, Jesus further clarified this principle of selfless love when He said, *"It is more blessed (makes one happier and more to be envied) to give than to receive."* He, certainly, should know about giving. He gave His very life for us. In John 15:13, Jesus also said, *"No one has greater love [no one has shown stronger affection] than to lay down (give up) his own life for his friends."*

Jesus loved you, and laid down His life for you; now you, in turn, are free to love others, and thereby continue the cycle of love. First John 4:19 tells us *we love Him because He first loved us*. God started this whole process. Because He loved us, despite our sins and while we were still in the state caused by our sins, we are free to love. As we freely love others, we can know with confidence that God promises to bless us in return. So, as God admonishes us, let's make love our great quest. Let it give your life dignity and meaning so that at the end of your life, the Lord can say to you proudly, *"Well done, you upright (honorable, admirable) and faithful servant!"* (Matthew 25:21)

～ Life Application ～

1. In 1 Corinthians 14:1, God instructs us to make love our great quest. What does that mean to you? How will it affect your life from now on?

   _____

   _____

   _____

   _____

2. According to 1 Corinthians 13:5, why are we able to love others selflessly?

   _____

   _____

   _____

3. Read Luke 6:38. Describe how things you give away are given back to you.

   _____

   _____

   _____

4. Do you think Jesus was a good example of selfless love? Why or why not?

   _____

   _____

   _____

   _____

~ Journal ~

Why does God want us to make love our aim or greatest quest? What can you do to implement this in your life today?

_____

_____

_____

_____

_____

_____

_____

_____

_____

_____

_____

_____

_____

_____

_____

_____

_____

_____

_____

Love Is A Call

~∾~

*All things work together and are [fitting into a plan]
for good to and for those who love God and are called
according to [His] design and purpose.*

Romans 8:28

~∾~

For many of us, life is nothing but a big mystery. We
walk around most of the time in a fog, wondering exactly
why we were put on this planet. Were you aware that it
has never been God's plan for you to be confused and
dazed regarding your purpose in life? In John 10:10, Jesus
says that He came so you can *have and enjoy life, and
have it in abundance (to the full, till it overflows.)* That
sounds wonderful, but you can't really enjoy life if you're
in a state of confusion, can you?

Perhaps you've talked with guidance counselors or taken
personality profiles, and you're still not exactly sure what
you're supposed to be doing with your life. Is it possible
your lack of direction is grounded in the fact that you don't
know your Designer very well? How can you know what
you're best suited for, or where you'll be most fulfilled, if
you don't know the One who designed you in the first place?

Part of God's purpose in loving you is that He has a
calling for you. He has designed a one-of-a-kind role that
no one but you can fill. Every facet of your personality
— the twinkle in your eye, the brightness of your smile

— was designed by God for a specific purpose. His plan was never for you to merely exist. On the contrary, God loves you and is calling you into a relationship with Him for the purpose of revealing His grand design for your life. If your earthly parents love you and want the best for you, imagine how much more your Heavenly Father wants to see you operating at your very best! He wants you to have a wonderful, abundant life, full of joy and peace. But that's only possible by knowing Him and experiencing His great love personally. When you realize just how much God loves you, and that He planned your life with a one-of-a-kind purpose, all the confusion will disappear.

Ephesians 1:17-19 says God will *grant you a spirit of wisdom and revelation [of insight into mysteries and secrets] in the [deep and intimate] knowledge of Him. By having the eyes of your heart flooded with light, so that you can know and understand the hope to which He has called you, and how rich is His glorious inheritance in the saints (His set-apart ones), and [so that you can know and understand] what is the immeasurable and unlimited and surpassing greatness of His power in and for* [you]. Not only has God called you, He will give you wisdom and understanding so you won't be mystified about your life, but will have a clear picture of your purpose; then you will know and understand the vastness of His plan for you as well as His power to fulfill it through you. Won't you answer His call by opening your heart to Him and letting Him begin this wonderful work in you?

~ Life Application ~

1. Read Romans 8:28. For whom do all things work together?

   _____

   _____

   _____

   _____

   _____

2. Romans 11:29 says: *God's gifts and His call are irrevocable.
   [He never withdraws them when once they are given, and He
   does not change His mind about those to whom He gives His
   grace or to whom He sends His call.]* What does it mean
   that God's call is "irrevocable?" Has His plan for you
   changed? Do you think He wants you to fulfill it?

   _____

   _____

   _____

   _____

   _____

3. How can loving God help you have a fulfilled life?

   _____

   _____

   _____

   _____

   _____

~ Journal ~

Did you know that God had a divine calling on your life?
Do you have any idea what that plan might be? Write down
your thoughts.

_____

_____

_____

_____

_____

_____

_____

_____

_____

_____

_____

_____

_____

_____

_____

_____

_____

_____

_____

Love Is A Gift

~≈~

For God so greatly loved and dearly prized the world that He [even] gave up His only begotten (unique) Son, so that whoever believes in (trusts in, clings to, relies on) Him shall not perish (come to destruction, be lost) but have eternal (everlasting) life. For God did not send the Son into the world in order to judge (to reject, to condemn, to pass sentence on) the world, but that the world might find salvation and be made safe and sound through Him.

John 3:16-17

~≈~

God wants to have a loving, interactive, obstacle-free relationship with us. But because God is a righteous, pure and holy God, He cannot fellowship with sin (wrongdoing). He can only fellowship with righteousness (conformity to God's will in thought, word and deed). God is so wonderful, however, that He not only provides a way to get rid of the obstacle between Himself and us, He also helps us keep that obstacle from coming back. God enables us to do this by offering us a free gift, His Son, Jesus Christ, Who is the only one who can break down the barrier between us and God caused by sin.

Romans 3:23 says *all have sinned and are falling short of the honor and glory which God bestows and receives.* You see, all of us, except Jesus, have sinned and fallen short of God's best for our lives. God, therefore, gave Jesus, His Son, as a sacrifice or substitute for us, to pay the price that we should have paid for our sin. In John 1:29, Jesus is called the *Lamb of God, Who takes away the sin of the world.* Jesus is the spotless lamb of God, the substitute for us, who paid the price for our sin. He did this by dying on the cross in our place, paying once and for all, for the sin of the world. Because of His death and resurrection, you are able to walk in fellowship with God.

But how do we accept God's gift to us? Romans 10:9 says *if you acknowledge and confess with your lips that Jesus is Lord and in your heart believe (adhere to, trust in, and rely on the truth) that God raised Him from the dead, you will be saved.* Jesus' death and resurrection paved the way for you to have eternal fellowship with God.

When we trust in and rely on Jesus, there is no longer a barrier between us and God. His power is then totally available to us, unhindered, to help us fulfill that for which He has called us. We can then start the process of knowing true love — God's love — which will enable us not only to begin to receive love, but to offer this very same gift of love to others.

～ Life Application ～

1. Read John 3:16. What must you do to have eternal life?

    _____

    _____

    _____

    _____

2. According to this scripture, why did God send Jesus into the world?

    _____

    _____

    _____

    _____

3. Read Romans 3:23. In what way do you think you may have sinned and fallen short of God's glory (His best for you)?

    _____

    _____

    _____

    _____

4. Read Romans 10:9. What do you have to do to be saved?

    _____

    _____

    _____

    _____

~ Journal ~

Have you done according to Romans 10:9 and confessed with your lips that Jesus is Lord and that God raised Him from the dead? If not, do so now, in the form of a written confession. Write down any thoughts you might have, as well.

_____

_____

_____

_____

_____

_____

_____

_____

_____

_____

_____

_____

_____

_____

_____

_____

_____

Love Is Pure

~~≈~~

Who shall go up into the mountain of the Lord? Or who shall stand in His Holy Place? He who has clean hands and a pure heart.

Psalm 24:3-4

~~≈~~

God made an interactive and loving relationship with Him available to us through our acceptance of Jesus Christ. But sometimes, even with Jesus in our hearts we make mistakes and miss God's best for us. Matthew 5:8 says: *Blessed (happy, enviably fortunate, and spiritually prosperous)…are the pure in heart, for they shall see God.* When we miss God's best for us, it's because we've lost focus and sight of God in our lives. In order to restore that sight, to actively see God working in our lives again, we've got to have a pure heart before Him. But again, if we've done anything in thought, word or deed that's not in line with God's perfect plan for us, it becomes an obstacle in our relationship with God. This obstacle is called "sin," which is a word derived from an old archery term meaning to "miss the mark." When we've sinned, we've missed God's bulls-eye, His very best for us.

Now, it really doesn't matter if you've sinned a little

or a lot. In fact, Romans 3:23 says all of us *have sinned and are falling short of the honor and glory which God bestows and receives.* All of us have fallen short and missed the mark at times. But the very good news is that God has made a way for us to be reinstated or restored to right relationship with Him; to get our hearts pure again. First John 1:9 says *if we [freely] admit that we have sinned and confess our sins, He [God] is faithful and just (true to His own nature and promises) and will forgive our sins [dismiss our lawlessness] and [continuously] cleanse us from all unrighteousness [everything not in conformity to His will in purpose, thought and action].* Here we see God has made a way for us to be completely restored to Him in the event we fall out of fellowship with Him because of sin. All we must do is freely admit that we've blown it, and allow Him to cleanse our hearts. It's that simple.

So, the next time you feel any distance between you and God, or if you've hit a snag, check your heart and confess whatever you find to God. Allow Him to cleanse and purify your heart so you're right back on track with His best plan for your life, headed for the bulls-eye. Make this a lifestyle. As you do, you'll see God actively involved in your life. Remember, it's the pure in heart who are able to see a pure and holy God.

~ Life Application ~

1. Read Psalm 24:3-4. Who does it say can go up to the mountain of God or stand in the holy place?

   _____

   _____

   _____

   _____

2. Matthew 5:8 expounds on this further. What do you think it means to "see God"?

   _____

   _____

   _____

3. Read 1 John 1:9. What do these verses tell us God will do for us if we confess our sins to Him?

   _____

   _____

   _____

4. What does "cleanse us from unrighteousness" mean?

   _____

   _____

   _____

~ Journal ~

What are some of the steps you need to take in order to keep a pure heart and clean hands before God?

_____

_____

_____

_____

_____

_____

_____

_____

_____

_____

_____

_____

_____

_____

_____

_____

_____

_____

_____

Love Is A Choice

~∽~

I have set before you life and death, the blessings and the curses; therefore choose life, that you and your descendants may live.

Deuteronomy 30:19

And if it seems evil to you to serve the Lord, choose for yourselves this day whom you will serve…but as for me and my house, we will serve the Lord.

Joshua 24:15

~∽~

In 1 Peter 2:9, God speaks of those whom He's called, and who have responded to His call, as *a chosen race, a royal priesthood, a dedicated nation, [God's] own purchased, special people, that you may set forth the wonderful deeds and display the virtues and perfections of Him Who called you out of darkness into His marvelous light.* God wants to show the world His wonderful plan through you, but He desires that you love and follow Him of your own free will. Remember, love, as we've seen in 1 Corinthians 13:7, does not demand its own way.

God's love is such that He doesn't force you to serve Him, but allows you to make a choice. Deuteronomy 30:19 speaks of blessings and cursings. Maybe you consider yourself blessed, or possibly, your life has derailed. Proverbs 29:18 says: *Where there is no vision* [no redemptive revelation of God], the people perish; but he who keeps the law [of God, which includes that of man] — blessed (happy, fortunate, and enviable) is he. God has certain rules of conduct for us to follow in order for us to be blessed. If we make the choice to follow them, God has good plans for us. In Jeremiah 29:11, God says, *"For I know, the thoughts and plans that I have for you…thoughts and plans for welfare and peace and not for evil, to give you hope in your final outcome."* God has always had a wonderful plan for you, but you must tap into that plan; it's not automatic. It's your choice; go it alone in life, hit-or-miss; or have God right there guiding and helping you every step of the way through His Word.

In John 10:10, Jesus says, *"The thief comes only in order to steal and kill and destroy. I came that they may have and enjoy life, and have it in abundance (to the full, till it overflows.)"* Without God, your life is up for grabs — it's a 50-50 proposition. You may be one of the fortunate few who, for a season, seem to be blessed; but you could also end up one of the sad cases whose life just doesn't seem to work out. God's desire is for you to have an abundant, blessed life. He can only promise that to you if you'll let Him take an active part. As Joshua 24:15 says, you have a decision to make: abundance or lack; success or failure. Whom will you serve? The choice is yours.

~ Life Application ~

1. How would you describe God's plan for your life, according to Jeremiah 29:11?

    _____

    _____

    _____

2. Read Proverbs 29:18. What does the blessed, happy and fortunate person do?

    _____

    _____

    _____

3. In a dictionary, look up the definition of the words "blessing" and "cursing." What do they mean?

    _____

    _____

    _____

4. Read Deuteronomy 28:1-14 in your Bible. Write down a few of the blessings God promises to those who obey Him. Then read Deuteronomy 28:15-45, and write down some of the curses.

    _____

    _____

    _____

    _____

~ Journal ~

Until now, were you aware that God offers you a choice as to the outcome of your life? Now that you've seen the choices, which will you choose, blessings or curses? Write down any thoughts you might have.

_____

_____

_____

_____

_____

_____

_____

_____

_____

_____

_____

_____

_____

_____

_____

_____

_____

_____

_____

Love Is A Relationship

~∾~

God is love, and he who dwells and continues in love dwells and continues in God, and God dwells and continues in him.

1 John 4:16

~∾~

For a relationship between two people to flourish, there must be ongoing interaction between the parties involved. The same is true in our relationship with God. It isn't a one-time event; it's a continual process. For it to be successful, we must invest time and energy into it.

First John 4:16 says that when we dwell in love we dwell in God, and He dwells in us. In Ephesians 3:17, Paul says, *"May Christ through your faith [actually] dwell (settle down, abide, make His permanent home) in your hearts! May you be rooted deep in love and founded securely on love."* How do we get rooted and grounded in love? First of all, through faith, which, simply put, is trusting God.

Romans 10:17 tells us *faith comes by hearing [what is told], and what is heard comes by the preaching [of the message that came from the lips] of Christ (the Messiah Himself).* The more of God's Word we hear, the more faith we have. Through this faith then, Jesus is able to dwell more permanently in our hearts.

We also get grounded in love by renewing our minds. Ephesians 4:23-24 tells us: *Be constantly renewed in the spirit of your mind [having a fresh mental and spiritual attitude], and put on the new nature (the regenerate self) created in God's image, [Godlike] in true righteousness and holiness.* As we continue to hear God's Word, our thoughts and mental images begin to change to conform to the way God sees and does things. We no longer think like our old selves, rather, we begin to think like God. In this way, God is made more and more at home in our hearts.

Another way to get rooted and grounded in love is to meditate on God's Word. The more you know about God, the more you see what a wonderful, loving, merciful God He is; the more you dwell on good thoughts you've gleaned from the Word, the more you'll become rooted in love, because God is love; the more you know His Word, the more you become like Him; the more you are like Him, the more you will walk in love. It's a wonderful cycle. The more you meditate on the Word of God — thinking about it, picturing it, seeing yourself doing it — the more you'll be transformed into the image and likeness of Jesus. He will start to take a larger and larger place in your heart. Your old self will start to fade away, and you'll become a brand new person.

Your relationship with God, as well as all of your other relationships, will prosper.

~ Life Application ~

1. Read 1 John 4:16 again. What does it mean to "dwell in love"?

_____

_____

_____

_____

2. How does one continue in love?

_____

_____

_____

3. According to Romans 10:17, how to we get faith? Is this a one-time experience?

_____

_____

_____

_____

4. According to Ephesians 4:23-24 what does it mean to renew your mind?

_____

_____

_____

_____

~ Journal ~

Read Ephesians 3:17-20. Then read 1 Corinthians 2:9. Write down some of the reasons a relationship with God is important. What are the benefits to you? What kind of things do you imagine God has prepared for you?

_____

_____

_____

_____

_____

_____

_____

_____

_____

_____

_____

_____

_____

_____

_____

_____

_____

_____

Love Has A Plan

~⊰⊱~

Eye has not seen and ear has not heard and has not entered into the heart of man, [all that] God has prepared (made and keeps ready) for those who love Him [who hold Him in affectionate reverence, promptly obeying Him and gratefully recognizing the benefits He has bestowed.]

1 Corinthians 2:9

~⊰⊱~

Many of us think that love exists for the purpose of pleasant companionship and procreation. Although this is true, God had an even bigger agenda when He admonished us to pursue love. According to 1 Corinthians 2:9, love is the key to unlocking God's future plans for us. As we continue on our quest for love, as we love God and others, God's full intention for our lives will enter into our hearts. We'll start to see His "big picture" for us.

Motivational speakers often tell us to remind ourselves: "If it's to be, it's up to me." We think that it's our responsibility to pursue and make our own goals and dreams happen. But what we sometimes fail to realize is that the best dreams and goals for our life are actually activated by a loving relationship with God. God reciprocates His love to us through others. As we learn about, and continue to love God and our neighbor, God will put people in our path who will actually be instrumental in our future. Different opportunities will arise in which He will bless us through others as we make love our great quest. Love then, can be said to open doors of opportunity for us.

In Revelation 3:8, Jesus is speaking to a church that loved Him above anything else. He said, *"I have set before you a door wide open which no one is able to shut; I know that you have but little power, and yet you have kept My Word and guarded My message."* These people loved God; they obeyed and kept His message and continued in their relationship with Him. God opened doors for them through which they walked to fulfill His perfect plan.

In Psalm 91:14-16, God says: *Because he [the person who loves God] has set his love upon Me, therefore will I deliver him; I will set him on high, because He knows and understands. My name [has a personal knowledge of My mercy, love, and kindness — trusts and relies on Me, knowing I will never forsake him, no, never.] He shall call upon Me, and I will answer him; I will be with him in trouble, I will deliver him and honor him. With long life will I satisfy him and show him My salvation."* This is His perfect plan for you. As you continue in your loving relationship with God, He promises many wonderful things for you, including a satisfied life. This satisfaction will be yours because you'll know that God has planned only good things for you in the future.

~ Life Application ~

1. Jeremiah 29:11 says: *I [God] know the thoughts and plans that I have for you, says the Lord, thoughts and plans for welfare and peace and not for evil, to give you hope in your final outcome.* In your own words, describe the kind of plan God has for your life.

    _____

    _____

    _____

2. What do you think an "open door" means, according to Revelation 3:8?

    _____

    _____

    _____

3. Read Psalm 91:14-16 again. What does God say He will do for those who love Him?

    _____

    _____

    _____

4. According to 1 Corinthians 2:9, what are some of the characteristics of the person who loves God?

    _____

    _____

    _____

~ Journal ~

Read 1 Corinthians 2:9 again. Ponder it. What does it lead you to believe about the scope of God's plan for your life? Does that change your love for Him in any way?

_____

_____

_____

_____

_____

_____

_____

_____

_____

_____

_____

_____

_____

_____

_____

_____

_____

_____

_____

Love Prepares A Path

~∾~

We are God's [own] handiwork (His workmanship) recreated in Christ Jesus, [born anew] that we may do those good works which God predestined (planned beforehand) for us [taking paths which He prepared ahead of time], that we should walk in them [living the good life which He prearranged and made ready for us to live.]

Ephesians 2:10

~∾~

Life is definitely a journey. For some, it's like a vacation full of pleasant sights and exciting encounters. For others, the journey is more treacherous: Danger lies around every curve; every encounter threatens survival. Why the difference? Is one path easier than another?

There are pitstops and pitfalls along almost any path. The difference is in the preparation for the journey. If the traveler is unprepared, what should be an easy path can be treacherous; and a difficult path can be made infinitely easier if we are ready for it. The Titanic's tragedy was not that it hit an iceberg, but that it was unprepared. It was lack of preparation that cost the lives of so many people.

Perhaps you're asking yourself, "How can I possibly

know the future?" The truth is, you can't. But the Good News is, there is Someone Who knows the future and has already done all the preparation for you. The part you play is this: trusting God. Proverbs 3:5-6 tells us: *Lean on, trust in, and be confident in the Lord with all your heart and mind and do not rely on your own insight or understanding. In all your ways know, recognize, and acknowledge Him, and He will direct and make straight and plain your paths.* That should take a load off your shoulders. Your job is simply to trust God.

Psalm 16:11 says of God: *You will show me the path of life; in Your presence is fullness of joy.* You, in your own frail little mind can't possibly know what lies around the bend for you, for you the future's a big mystery. But not to God! Philippians 1:6 says: *He* [God] *Who began a good work in you will continue until the day of Jesus Christ [right up to the time of His return], developing [that good work] and perfecting and bringing it to full completion in you.* The future is God's responsibility, not yours. So, don't sweat the small stuff. Since you don't know exactly what lies around the bend for you, trust in God. He'll make your path plain and He'll be there every step of the way to help you complete your journey.

~ Life Application ~

1. According to Psalm 16:11, who will show you the path of your life? What will you experience in His presence?

   _____

   _____

   _____

2. Were you aware that God had a path for you to walk? For what purpose were we recreated in Christ? According to Ephesians 2:10, what kind of life does God want us to lead?

   _____

   _____

   _____

3. Using your Bible or dictionary for clarification, look up the word "trust." What does it mean to trust in God?

   _____

   _____

   _____

4. Why does Proverbs 3:5 say not to lean on your own understanding concerning your future? Do you think God might know something that you don't know? Write down your thoughts.

   _____

   _____

   _____

~ Journal ~

Read Proverbs 3:5-6 again. What are some things you can do so that God will direct your path? What are some things you can do to trust God more with your future?

_____

_____

_____

_____

_____

_____

_____

_____

_____

_____

_____

_____

_____

_____

_____

_____

_____

_____

_____

_____

Love Is A Guide

~∾~

I have not turned aside from Your ordinances, for You Yourself have taught me....Through your precepts I get understanding....Your word is a lamp to my feet and a light to my path.

Psalm 119:102, 104, 105

~∾~

A long time ago, three kings were able to find the baby Messiah because they were wise enough to follow a star. Their wisdom was not so much in their intelligence as it was in their obedience to follow the light. Although that particular star may no longer shine in the heavens today, God has given us our own "guiding light" to follow.

Matthew 4:16 says that *the people who sat (dwelt enveloped) in darkness have seen a great Light, and for those who sat in the land and shadow of death Light has dawned.* Perhaps you were one of these people. At one point, your life may have seemed shrouded in darkness; there seemed to be no light at the end of the tunnel for you. Now, however, because you are a citizen of God's kingdom, you no longer dwell in darkness, but are part of the kingdom of light. Psalm 119:102-105 tells us that through studying God's Word — as you're doing right now — you'll gain greater insight and understanding into life. You'll no longer walk in confusion, like a blind person, but will have your eyes fully opened to life. Psalm 36:9 says: *With You* [God] *is the fountain of life; in Your light do we see light.*

God is so good that not only does He give us His Word as a light, He also gives us Jesus as a personal guide, a living example of God in the flesh, to follow. God is so gracious to us that He has left all the guesswork out of following Him. In John 8:12, Jesus spoke of Himself saying, *"I am the Light of the world. He who follows Me will not be walking in the dark, but will have the Light which is Life."* You see, Jesus is not only the Light, He is also Life itself.

Hebrews 1:3 says of Jesus: *He is the sole expression of the glory of God [the Light-being, the out-raying or radiance of the divine], and He is the perfect imprint and very image of [God's] nature, upholding and maintaining and guiding and propelling the universe by His mighty word of power.* Jesus is the perfect imprint and image of God's nature. When we take a look at Jesus, we see God. He upholds, maintains, guides and propels the universe — which is no small feat — and at the same time, He also wants to guide your life. Take time to read His Word and follow His example by obeying His instructions. In that way, as you follow His guiding light, you'll gain greater understanding and will be able to walk in that abundant life He came to give you.

～ Life Application ～

1. In Psalm 119:102-105, who does the teaching? What is the light?

   _____

   _____

   _____

   _____

2. How does one get understanding?

   _____

   _____

   _____

   _____

3. What does John 8:12 tell you to do to stay out of the darkness?

   _____

   _____

   _____

   _____

4. What two things does this verse say Jesus is? What does that mean to you?

   _____

   _____

   _____

   _____

~ Journal ~

Meditate on Hebrews 1:3. Can you trust Jesus to guide your future? Do you think He can handle the job?

_____

_____

_____

_____

_____

_____

_____

_____

_____

_____

_____

_____

_____

_____

_____

_____

_____

_____

Love Believes The Best

~≈~

Love…is ever ready to believe the best of every person,
its hopes are fadeless under all circumstances.

1 Corinthians 13:7

~≈~

Have you ever had a person in your life who thought you could do no wrong and saw only the potential you had inside of you? They may have encouraged you to "be all you could be." They believed in you, rooted for you, thought you were special. They gave you confidence in yourself.

Well, God is the greatest motivator of them all. Philippians 4:8 gives us a clue as to how God thinks about us: *Whatever is true, whatever is worthy of reverence and is honorable and seemly, whatever is just, whatever is pure, whatever is lovely and lovable, whatever is kind and winsome and gracious, if there is any virtue and excellence, if there is anything worthy of praise, think on and weigh and take account of these things [fix your minds on them].* All of us have flaws and imperfections. We've all made mistakes. But when God looks at us, believe it or not, He's not looking at those things. In Song of Solomon 4:7, the

Shepherd, who represents Jesus, says, *"O my love, how beautiful you are! There is no flaw in you!"* God doesn't focus on your flaws and imperfections; He sees only what is praiseworthy in you, the best that you are now and will be in the future.

As we walk in love, the Lord dwells in us and we dwell in Him. We become united with Him. Ephesians 5:29-30 says *no man ever hated his own flesh, but nourishes and carefully protects and cherishes it, as Christ does the church, because we are members (parts) of His body.*

God cherishes you because you are part of Himself. When He looks at you, He sees Jesus.

James 1:17 further substantiates this idea: *Every good gift and every perfect…gift is from above.* You see, you came from above and you are one of God's perfect gifts. And God doesn't make junk. The next time you're tempted to think the worst of yourself, remember that God only sees your potential. United with Him you have no flaws, only possibilities. In fact, Numbers 23:19 says: *God is not a man, that He should tell or act a lie.* Rest assured then, if God thinks you're great, that's all there is to it. No discussion!

∽ Life Application ∽

1. What do you think 1 Corinthians 13:7 means when it says that God's hopes are fadeless toward you?

   _____

   _____

   _____

   _____

   _____

   _____

2. What does Numbers 23:19 say about God's character?

   _____

   _____

   _____

   _____

   _____

   _____

3. What kind of things does Philippians 4:8 tell us to think about? Write them down.

   _____

   _____

   _____

   _____

   _____

   _____

~ Journal ~

Read Philippians 4:8, but this time, apply it to thoughts of yourself. For example, what is true about yourself? What is worthy of reverence about yourself, etc? Go through each area mentioned, noting these same good qualities in yourself. After you have done so, read them again, this time with the idea that this is how God thinks about you.

_____

_____

_____

_____

_____

_____

_____

_____

_____

_____

_____

_____

_____

_____

_____

Love Is A Destination

~∼~

Seek (aim at and strive after) first of all His kingdom and His righteousness (His way of doing and being right), and then all these things taken together will be given you besides.

Matthew 6:33

~∼~

Love is not only a person, it's a place where the King of Love dwells. First John 4:16 says: *God is love, and he who dwells and continues in love dwells and continues in God, and God dwells and continues in him.* This kingdom has its own system of operation. According to Matthew 6:33, we are to do things the way God does them, turning from our own way of doing things to God's way, operating on His principles. Matthew 7:21 gives us further insight into this by telling us Jesus said, *"Not everyone who says to Me, Lord, Lord, will enter the kingdom of heaven, but he who does the will of My Father Who is in heaven."* When we are obedient to do things God's way, we are operating in the kingdom of heaven here on earth.

Ephesians 3:17 says: *May Christ through your faith [actually] dwell (settle down, abide, make His permanent home) in your hearts.* God rules His kingdom from our hearts.

Ephesians 3:17 also says: *May you be rooted deep in love and founded securely on love.* We've got to be rooted deep in love in order for the King to rule His kingdom from our hearts.

Matthew 6:33 tells us that God wants first place, not last place, in our lives. In this way, He can guide us on our path and help us avoid many pitfalls. But we must do things the way He tells us to. It's one thing to ask God to help us; it's quite another to follow His instructions.

Matthew 6:33 follows a passage of scripture that tells us not to worry about food, clothing and shelter, because God will provide these things for us if we seek His kingdom first. This way of doing things is exactly the opposite of what we'd expect. The world tells us to save our money, not share with others, etc. God on the other hand, tells us to give things away if we want to be blessed. Luke 6:38, for example, says: *Give, and [gifts] will be given to you…For with the measure you deal out [with the measure you use when you confer benefits on others], it will be measured back to you.* It may not seem logical, but that's the way God's kingdom operates. So, allow yourself to be rooted and founded deeper and more securely on love. Seek God's kingdom, and His rule and reign in your heart. Follow His instructions. When you do so, He'll provide you with all the things you desire and you'll find yourself abiding permanently in the Kingdom of His love.

~ Life Application ~

1. According to Ephesians 3:17, from where does Jesus actually rule His kingdom?

    _____

    _____

    _____

    _____

2. According to the instructions of Matthew 6:33, how do you give further place to Jesus' rule in your heart?

    _____

    _____

    _____

3. Read Matthew 6:25-33. What will be added to you if you seek God's kingdom and do things His way?

    _____

    _____

    _____

4. What part, if any, does obedience play in doing things God's way?

    _____

    _____

    _____

    _____

~ Journal ~

How does doing Matthew 6:33 make Ephesians 3:17 more possible? What do you think it means to be rooted deeply in, and founded securely on, love?

_____

_____

_____

_____

_____

_____

_____

_____

_____

_____

_____

_____

_____

_____

_____

_____

_____

_____

_____

_____

Love Unites

~≈~

*Our Father Who is in heaven, hallowed (kept holy)
be Your name. Your kingdom come, Your will be done
on earth as it is in heaven.*

Matthew 6:9-10

~≈~

In Genesis 1:26 God said: *"Let Us [Father, Son, and
Holy Spirit] make mankind in Our image, after Our
likeness."* Love can be said then, to be made of three parts,
Father, Son and Holy Spirit, working in complete unity
and harmony with each other. What one part of the Godhead
does is exactly the same as the other. In fact, in John 10:30
Jesus said, *"I and the Father are One,"* and in John 12:45,
"Whoever sees Me sees Him Who sent Me." This principle of
unity plays a very important part in God's kingdom.

Jesus prayed in Matthew 6:9-10, that God's will would
be done on earth just as it would be done in heaven. If
we apply that scripture to unity, then walking in God's
love enables us to walk in unity here on earth. In fact, it
speaks of unity between heaven and earth. This principle
starts with us being united to God through obedience, in
fellowship with God. It also applies to you as an

individual. As you allow God to put the pieces of your life back together, you become unified, or whole. Your body, soul, mind and strength line up and you experience wholeness. As you become more whole or "holy" you then can reach out to others with God's love, and bring this unity to your relationships. This is called reconciliation.

Galatians 5:17 says: *the desires of the flesh are opposed to the [Holy] Spirit, and the [desires of the] Spirit are opposed to the flesh (godless human nature).* What fruits or desires does God's Spirit produce in us? Galatians 5:22 says they are: *love, joy (gladness), peace, patience (an even temper, forbearance), kindness, goodness (benevolence), faithfulness, gentleness (meekness, humility), self-control (self-restraint, continence).* These fruit bring about unity, fellowship and reconciliation with God and others.

God's desire is to have His will done on earth, in your life. As you walk in love and fellowship with God, you then become a co-laborer with Him in bringing peace, unity, fellowship and reconciliation to a world desperately in need of it.

～ Life Application ～

1. What does the word "unity" mean to you? How does it relate to the Godhead?

   _____

   _____

   _____

2. In John 12:45, what did Jesus mean when He said that He and the Father are one? Why is that important?

   _____

   _____

   _____

3. Read Galatians 5:17. Are the desires of the flesh in unity with the Holy Spirit?

   _____

   _____

   _____

4. Why do you think the fruit of the Spirit, in Galatians 5:22, produce unity?

   _____

   _____

5. Why does God want His will done on earth? How does that involve unity?

   _____

   _____

~ Journal ~

In Matthew 6:9-10, Jesus prayed that God's will would be done on earth as in heaven, uniting heaven and earth. How would more unity affect your life and the relationships you're involved in?

_____

_____

_____

_____

_____

_____

_____

_____

_____

_____

_____

_____

_____

_____

_____

_____

_____

_____

Love Equips

~∾~

But the Comforter (Counselor, Helper, Intercessor, Advocate, Strengthener, Standby), the Holy Spirit, Whom the Father will send in My name [in My place, to represent Me and act on My behalf], He will teach you all things. And He will cause you to recall (will remind you of, bring to your remembrance) everything I [Jesus] have told you.
                                                                    John 14:26

~∾~

God loves you very much. He knows that in order for you to fulfill His plan for your life you're going to need help, so He's provided it through the Holy Spirit, His representative on the earth. The Holy Spirit will not only teach you God's Word and ways, but will also provide you help anytime you need it. Here are some of the ways in which He does that:

He is your Comforter, available to soothe and console you and cheer you up when you're down or grieving. He's the fulfillment of Matthew 5:4: *Blessed…are those who mourn, for they shall be comforted!*

He is your Counselor, teacher and a guide. Psalm 119:24 says: *Your testimonies also are my delight and my counselors.*

He is your Helper, Someone Who comes alongside you when a task is too difficult. Psalm 46:1 says of Him: *God is our Refuge and Strength…a very present and well-proved help in trouble.*

He is your Intercessor, a Mediator between you and

God; a messenger from God to you, and from you to God. Romans 8:26-27 says: *The [Holy] Spirit comes to our aid and bears us up in our weakness...the Spirit intercedes and pleads [before God] in behalf of the saints according to and in harmony with God's will.*

He is your Advocate. He defends you against the devil and recommends you to God. He's like a heavenly lawyer, representing you to God, the Judge. *But if anyone should sin, we have an Advocate.* (1 John 2:1)

He is your Strengthener. He gives you the power to overcome sin and obstacles to your relationship with God. Ephesians 3:16 says: *May He [God] grant you out of the rich treasury of His glory to be strengthened and reinforced with mighty power in the inner man by the [Holy] Spirit.*

He is your Standby, a person you can rely on in an emergency, available to you at a moment's notice. Psalm 18:6, 17 says: *In my distress [when seemingly closed in] I called upon the Lord and cried to my God; He heard my voice out of His temple (heavenly dwelling place), and my cry came before Him, into His [very] ears...He delivered me from my strong enemy and from those who hated and abhorred me, for they were too strong for me.*

In conclusion then, the Holy Spirit equips you with everything you need in any situation. As Philippians 4:19 says: *My God will liberally supply (fill to the full) your every need according to His riches in glory in Christ Jesus.* No matter what you may need, whether comfort, counseling or help, it's available to you by way of the Comforter, God's Holy Spirit.

~ Life Application ~

1. List a few of the names given the Holy Spirit in (John 14:26). What does each mean to you?

   _____

   _____

   _____

   _____

   _____

   _____

2. According to this verse, what two other things does the Holy Spirit do?

   _____

   _____

   _____

   _____

   _____

3. Who sends the Holy Spirit? Who does He represent here on earth? How?

   _____

   _____

   _____

   _____

   _____

   _____

~ Journal ~

According to Luke 11:13, how do you receive the Holy Spirit? How can having the Holy Spirit impact your relationship with God and others?

_____

_____

_____

_____

_____

_____

_____

_____

_____

_____

_____

_____

_____

_____

_____

_____

_____

_____

Love Overcomes

~∾~

If your enemy is hungry, feed him; if he is thirsty, give him drink; for by so doing you will heap burning coals upon his head. Do not let yourself be overcome with evil, but overcome (master) evil with good.

Romans 12:20-21

~∾~

Because of His generous, giving nature, Jesus offers us abundant life. But in John 10:10, He speaks of another, whose nature is not so generous: *"The thief comes only in order to steal and kill and destroy."* Who is this thief Jesus is describing? First Peter 5:8 plainly tells us: *Be well balanced (temperate, sober of mind), be vigilant and cautious at all times; for that enemy of yours, the devil, roams around like a lion roaring [in fierce hunger], seeking someone to seize upon and devour.* Here on earth, we have an enemy, the devil. He is described as a thief who comes to steal, kill and destroy. He is the author of all evil.

Sometimes, we are deceived by the devil into thinking that people are our enemies. But the truth is, it's the devil working behind the scenes, through them. Ephesians 6:12 tells us: *We are not wrestling with flesh and blood [contending only with physical opponents], but against...the powers, against [the master spirits who are] the world rulers of this present darkness, against the spirit forces of wickedness in the heavenly (supernatural) sphere.*

Romans 12:20-21 gives us the key to overcoming evil,

and that is, by doing good. As citizens of God's kingdom, we are subject to the highest law there is — the law of love, which supercedes all other laws in all other kingdoms. Why is this law so powerful it will overcome evil? First Corinthians 13:8 tells us: *Love never fails [never fades out or becomes obsolete or comes to an end].* Yes, evil does exist, but only for a season. Love, however, is eternal.

In John 16:33, Jesus assures us of this: *"Be of good cheer [take courage; be confident, certain, undaunted]! For I have overcome the world. [I have deprived it of power to harm you and have conquered it for you.]"* When Jesus paid the price on Calvary, He overcame evil on our behalf.

How then do we enforce Jesus' victory over evil? James 4:7-8 says: *Be subject to God. Resist the devil [stand firm against him], and he will flee from you. Come close to God and He will come close to you.* As we draw close to God, as we study and meditate on His Word, and renew our mind, His laws and love will become greater in our life. First Peter 5:9-10 describes this: *Withstand him* [the devil]; *be firm in faith [against his onset — rooted, established, strong, immovable, and determined]….and after you have suffered a little while…Christ Jesus will, Himself, complete and make you what you ought to be, establish and ground you securely, and strengthen, and settle you.*

So, the next time you're faced with an opportunity to overcome evil, do so with the greatest spiritual weapon given to us by God — love. Draw close to God; resist the devil; and shower your enemies with kindness. Let Jesus make you what you ought to be as you are settled and grounded in Him. Most of all, remember, love never fails!

~ Life Application ~

1. According to John 10:10 and 1 Peter 5:8, who is your enemy and what does he do?

   _____

   _____

   _____

2. According to Ephesians 6:12, who are we wrestling with? Are they flesh and blood opponents? In what realm do they operate?

   _____

   _____

   _____

3. Read John 16:33 and 1 Corinthians 13:8. According to these scriptures, why can you be confident that the devil is no match for you?

   _____

   _____

   _____

4. What do James 4:7-8 and 1 Peter 5:9-10 tell us to do to overcome our enemy?

   _____

   _____

   _____

   _____

~ Journal ~

Read Romans 12:20-21 again. Now that you know a little bit about God's weapon against evil, describe some ways you will implement it in your life.

_____

_____

_____

_____

_____

_____

_____

_____

_____

_____

_____

_____

_____

_____

_____

_____

_____

_____

_____

_____

Love Is A Power

~≈~

God is able to make all grace (every favor and earthly blessing) come to you in abundance, so that you may always and under all circumstances and whatever the need be self-sufficient [possessing enough to require no aid or support and furnished in abundance for every good work and charitable donation].

2 Corinthians 9:8

~≈~

With the realization that God has a wonderful plan for your life often comes the intimidating question, "But what if I fail?" We somehow believe that even though it is God Who has called us, we are on our own when it comes to fulfilling His plan. But have no fear! God has a power available to help you. It's called grace.

Because God is love and He believes the best, when He looks at you He does so in much the same way as a parent looks at a beloved child. This is called "favor." Matthew 7:11 gives us an example of this: *If you then, evil as you are, know how to give good and advantageous gifts to your children, how much more will your Father Who is in heaven [perfect as He is] give good and advantageous things to those who keep on asking Him!* It is God's desire to give you good things that benefit you. In fact, one definition of grace is "the extremely diverse powers and gifts granted to Christians by unmerited favor." So, grace includes both God's power and the gifts that God makes available to you. Keep in mind, these are not something you earn; they are unmerited and undeserved powers and gifts.

But how do you receive this grace? James 4:6 tells us: [God] *gives us more and more grace (power of the Holy Spirit, to meet…evil tenden[cies] and all others fully). That is why… God sets Himself against the proud and haughty, but gives grace [continually] to the lowly (those who are humble enough to receive it).* We receive God's grace by being humble, by not thinking highly of ourselves, or thinking that we deserve His favor. There is no way we could ever be good enough or do enough to deserve God's favor. When we realize this, then we are humble enough to receive it, and God is able to help us with whatever we need in the situation.

Philippians 4:19 also tells us a little bit about God's grace: *My God will liberally supply (fill to the full) your every need according to His riches in glory in Christ Jesus.* God is our Source. He has plenty of resources available to help us. But how do we access this supply of grace? James 1:5 says: *If any of you is deficient in wisdom, let him ask of the giving God [Who gives] to everyone liberally and ungrudgingly, without reproaching or faultfinding, and it will be given him.* Although this passage is about wisdom, the same principle holds true: you receive by asking — and it's very wise to ask for grace!

So, the next time you need something from God, humble yourself and ask Him for it. His Word promises that He will supply all your needs according to His riches in glory. It doesn't matter whether you need strength, wisdom, or finances, He says that He will give it to you ungrudgingly and without nitpicking and faultfinding. Trust that He is true to His Word. Watch, and He will supply your every need with His abundant, unmerited favor called grace.

~ Life Application ~

1. According to James 4:6, what is the definition of "grace"?

   _____

   _____

   _____

   _____

2. Why is grace called "unmerited favor"?

   _____

   _____

   _____

3. In what areas of your life could you use more grace (especially if the definition is "the power of the Holy Spirit...to meet evil tendencies")? Were you aware that this power was available to you to overcome in these areas?

   _____

   _____

   _____

4. What do you need to do, according to Matthew 7:11, James 1:5 and 4:6, to receive God's grace?

   _____

   _____

   _____

   _____

~ Journal ~

Read Matthew 7:11 again. Since grace is one of God's good and perfect gifts to us, write down some areas in your life where you could use this power. Now ask God for it and watch what happens.

_____

_____

_____

_____

_____

_____

_____

_____

_____

_____

_____

_____

_____

_____

_____

_____

_____

_____

_____

Love Speaks The Truth

~*~

The sum of Your word is truth [the total of the full meaning of all Your individual precepts]; and every one of Your righteous decrees endures forever.

Psalm 119:160

~*~

Not only is God love, He is also the Truth. John 17:17 says of God's Word: *Your Word is Truth.* In an age when it's hard to distinguish what's right from what's wrong, it's nice to know there is still someone you can count on to tell you the absolute truth.

Numbers 23:19 says of God and His Word: *God is not a man, that He should tell or act a lie, neither the son of man, that He should feel repentance or compunction [for what He has promised]. Has He said and shall He not do it? Or has He spoken and shall He not make it good?* If God tells us something, it's a done deal. Second Corinthians 1:20 says: *As many as are the promises of God, they all find their Yes [answer] in Him [Christ].* All God's promises to us are "Yes" if we believe them. God's not a liar, and He doesn't change His mind.

When you became a citizen of God's kingdom, His Spirit became alive in you. Now, your assignment — if you choose to accept it — is to walk out your salvation; to learn more about God's kingdom and His way of doing things. You do this by agreeing with God's Word, which is Truth. When you agree with and speak God's Word, you speak the truth. For example, in John 10:10, Jesus says, *"I came that they may have and enjoy life, and have it in abundance (to the full, till it overflows)."* That's a promise to you. How then, do you agree with this promise? First, you study and meditate on it (roll it over in your mind, until the picture becomes a reality in your heart and you believe it wholeheartedly). Then, you speak it. By so doing you agree with the truth of God's Word. As you speak it, you will start to experience that abundant life God promised you.

The more you come into agreement with the truth of God's Word, the more victory you'll have in your life. This isn't an overnight event; it's a process which takes place over a period of time. Since it also involves renewing your mind, it will take time for you to replace your old way of thinking with God's way of doing things and being right. The process, however, is worth the effort, because God says in Isaiah 55:11: *"So shall My word be that goes forth out of My mouth; it shall not return to Me void [without producing any effect, useless], but it shall accomplish that which I please and purpose, and it shall prosper in the thing for which I sent it."* God's Word always accomplishes what it is sent out to do. When we agree with God by believing and speaking His Word, the same truth applies to us.

The next time you study and meditate on God's Word, remember that it's the Truth. When you pray, remember that He is faithful to His promises, and His Word will not return void, but will do what it's sent forth to do. Then, agree with His Word in your heart; speak it; and watch as God goes to work fulfilling His promises on your behalf.

~ Life Application ~

1. According to Numbers 23:19, why can you trust in the Word of God?

   _____

   _____

   _____

   _____

   _____

2. What steps must you take in order to agree with a promise of God?

   _____

   _____

   _____

   _____

   _____

3. What does 2 Corinthians 1:20 say is true about God's Word (His promises)?

   _____

   _____

   _____

   _____

   _____

~ Journal ~

Write 2 Corinthians 1:20, Isaiah 55:11, and three more promises of God you can agree with. Begin to meditate on them, and speak them daily.

_____

_____

_____

_____

_____

_____

_____

_____

_____

_____

_____

_____

_____

_____

_____

_____

_____

_____

_____

Love Is Trustworthy

~❧~

Lean on, trust in, and be confident in the Lord with all your heart and mind and do not rely on your own insight or understanding. In all your ways, know, recognize and acknowledge Him, and He will direct and make straight and plain your paths.

Proverbs 3:5-6

~❧~

God is worthy of our trust because of the great love He has for us. If, as a child, you trusted your earthly parents to take care of you because you knew they loved you, how much more should you trust your heavenly Father? Jesus said, in Mark 10:14-15, *"Allow the children to come to Me — do not forbid or prevent or hinder them — for to such belongs the kingdom of God. Truly, I tell you, whoever does not receive and accept and welcome the kingdom of God like a little child [does] positively shall not enter it at all."* In order for us to fully receive the kingdom of God, we must have a childlike trust. Because God is love, because He does not lie, He is completely worthy of our trust. Human beings sometimes betray our trust, but God doesn't. He does what He says He's going to do. All He asks is that you trust Him.

Deuteronomy 33:27 says: *The eternal God is your refuge and dwelling place, and underneath are the everlasting arms.* We are to trust God in the same way that a small child who jumps into a pool knows (believes and expects) her daddy will catch her. But how do we do this, especially if we're distrustful because of past experiences?

The Word of God is full of God's promises to us. But we must renew our minds to them so that we can take God's Word at face value. Romans 12:2 tells us: *Do not be conformed to this world (this age), [fashioned after and adapted to its external, superficial customs], but be transformed (changed) by the [entire] renewal of your mind [by its new ideals and attitude], so that you may prove [for yourselves] what is the good and acceptable and perfect will of God…[in His sight for you]*. As you learn more about God, you'll be able to trust Him more because you will better understand His heart toward you. The world may tell you not to trust anyone, but God says, "Trust Me." The world may tell you not to love anymore because it hurts too much, but God says, "Love Me and let Me love you." His words, hidden in your heart and renewed in your mind, will change your personality so that you can truly trust Him, and others, again.

First Corinthians 2:16 says: *We have the mind of Christ (the Messiah) and do hold the thoughts (feelings and purposes) of His heart*. As a believer in God, you do have the mind of Christ; and Jesus was not only the most trustworthy person to ever walk on this planet, but also the most trusting. On the cross, He trusted God the Father enough to put His life in God's hands. All God is asking us to do is to trust Him (by putting our hearts and lives in His hands just asJes us did), and to trust Jesus. If we do that, if we don't trust in our own understanding, but lean on Him, He promises to direct our paths and show us the way we should go.

God's hands are outstretched toward you. Be like that little child. Take a leap of faith!

~ Life Application ~

1. Read Mark 10:14-15. What does it mean to have childlike faith?

   _____

   _____

   _____

   _____

2. Read Romans 12:2. Why is it important to renew your mind to God's Word if you've been hurt by untrustworthy people in the past?

   _____

   _____

   _____

   _____

3. How does one renew one's mind?

   _____

   _____

   _____

   _____

4. According to Proverbs 3:5-6, what will God do for you if you trust in Him?

   _____

   _____

   _____

~ Journal ~

Jeremiah 17:7-8 says: *[Most] blessed is the man who believes in, trusts in, and relies on the Lord, and whose hope and confidence the Lord is.* Why is this person "most blessed"?

_____

_____

_____

_____

_____

_____

_____

_____

_____

_____

_____

_____

_____

_____

_____

_____

_____

_____

_____

_____

Love Is Dependable

~≈~

Blessed be the Lord, my Rock and my keen and firm Strength...my Steadfast Love and my Fortress, my High Tower and my Deliverer, my Shield and He in Whom I trust and take refuge.

Psalm 144:1-2

~≈~

Unlike some of the loves we may have had in our lives, who were not available for us when we needed them most, the love of God is totally dependable. In fact, the Lord, first of all, is called "The Rock." In Matthew 7:24-25, Jesus says, *"Everyone who hears these words of Mine and acts upon them [obeying them] will be like a sensible (prudent, practical, wise) man who built his house upon the rock. And the rain fell and the floods came and the winds blew and beat against that house; yet it did not fall, because it had been founded on the rock."* When we heed His words and obey them, we don't have to worry about the troubles that may come our way, because Jesus will take care of us. We are called sensible, prudent, practical and wise if we build our house upon Him, the Rock.

Psalm 46:1 tells us *God is our Refuge and Strength [mighty and impenetrable to temptation], a very present and well-proved help in trouble.* A secret place that you run to when you are in trouble. God is our Impenetrable Refuge; mighty and strong to deliver us and protect us from any enemy.

God is also described as our Steadfast Love. His love

is solid; firmly fixed in place or position. He's not going anywhere; He's at your side always because He loves you. There's no one like the Lord. Human beings, even when they love us, fail us at times. But the Lord doesn't; He is always dependable. In Romans 8:38-39 Paul said, *"I am persuaded beyond doubt (am sure) that neither death nor life, nor angels nor principalities, nor things impending and threatening nor things to come, nor powers, nor height nor depth, nor anything else in all creation will be able to separate us from the love of God which is in Christ Jesus our Lord."*

The Lord is also our Fortress, like a big castle or fort, with walls that surround and protect us. He is described as a High Tower — hidden away in the clouds, where we can see what's going on around us, but where we can't be seen and can't be touched by the enemy. Psalm 91:8 says: *Only a spectator shall you be [yourself inaccessible in the secret place of the Most High] as you witness the reward of the wicked.*

God is our Deliverer. Second Timothy 4:18 says: *The Lord will certainly deliver and draw me to Himself from every assault of evil. He will preserve and bring me safe unto His heavenly kingdom.* He is also our Shield; He protects us from whatever attacks the enemy may bring against us.

Finally, the Lord is the One in Whom you can trust and take refuge. Psalm 32:7 says of Him: *You are a hiding place for me; You, Lord, preserve me from trouble, You surround me with songs and shouts of deliverance.*

So, take God's Word at face value and know that He is Someone you can definitely depend on. He is always there, steady, dependable and strong. If you trust in God, be confident that, come what may, He's always dependable.

~ Life Application ~

1. Read Psalm 144:1-2. What does it mean to you that God is your Rock?

   _____

   _____

   _____

   _____

2. Read Psalm 46:1. Why is this a comfort to you?

   _____

   _____

   _____

   _____

3. According to Matthew 7:24-25, why is it wise to build your house upon the rock?

   _____

   _____

   _____

   _____

4. Read Romans 8:38. What *cannot* keep you from God's love?

   _____

   _____

   _____

   _____

~ Journal ~

Think about some people in your past or present who you consider dependable. What characteristics do these people have in common? How do you relate to them? Now, think about God being dependable. If He is as dependable as His Word says He is, how will that impact your relationship with Him from now on?

_____

_____

_____

_____

_____

_____

_____

_____

_____

_____

_____

_____

_____

_____

_____

_____

_____

_____

_____

Love Enables

~∼∾~

My grace (My favor and loving-kindness and mercy)
is enough for you...for My strength and power are
made perfect (fulfilled and completed) and show
themselves most effective in [your] weakness.
Therefore, I will all the more gladly glory in my
weaknesses and infirmities, that the strength and
power of Christ (the Messiah) may rest (yes, may pitch
a tent over and dwell) upon me!"

2 Corinthians 12:9

~∼∾~

No matter what situation you may be facing in your life, or what shortcomings you feel you have in fulfilling God's plan for your life, God's grace will get you through any situation. God doesn't do things the way we would, in fact His Word says: *God selected (deliberately chose) what in the world is foolish to put the wise to shame, and what the world calls weak to put the strong to shame* (1 Corinthians 1:27). When God chose a King for Israel, He deliberately chose David, the least of his brethren. And Jesus, the Savior of the world, was born in a stable, not in a palace as we would have expected the King of Kings to be.

God chooses weak or foolish things so none of us can boast; so credit will go where credit is due. This way, God gets the glory for our successes, not us — and rightly so. If we boast at all, Paul says, we should boast about our weaknesses, so that God receives the praise for our accomplishments. This certainly takes a load off of us! God can call any of us to do a job that is impossible for us to do in our own strength, and can give us everything we need to accomplish it. We don't have to have any special education or leaning toward it if God calls us to do it. We can know that God will help us every step of the way. In this way, we have no limits on our potential — because whether we have a talent in an area or not, God will enable us to do the job He has called us to do.

Many people fall short of God's plan for their lives, however, because they think they must be perfect in order to fulfill it. But the opposite is actually true. It is God Who perfects us. We don't have to do the perfecting. Isaiah 64:8 says: *Yet, O Lord, You are our Father; we are the clay, and You our Potter, and we all are the work of Your hand.* In 2 Corinthians 3:5 Paul says, *"Not that we are fit (qualified and sufficient in ability) of ourselves to...claim or count anything as coming from us, but our power and ability and sufficiency are from God."* It is God Who makes us fit to fulfill His plan for our lives. Our job is to cooperate with Him by acknowledging that we are weak; by studying and meditating on His Word, and by letting Him change and equip us from the inside out. His power works in us, and equips us to do the job He has called us to do.

So, the next time you're tempted to panic when God calls you to do a job you don't feel qualified for, remember Philippians 1:6: *He Who began a good work in you will continue until the day of Jesus Christ...developing [that good work] and perfecting and bringing it to full completion in you.*

~ Life Application ~

1. Read 2 Corinthians 12:9. Why was Paul so excited as to boast about his weaknesses?

   _____

   _____

   _____

   _____

2. Read 1 Corinthians 1:27. Why do you think God uses weak people to fulfill His plan? Can you think of any other Bible personalities who didn't seem equipped to do the job they were called for, but were able to with God's help?

   _____

   _____

   _____

   _____

3. According to 2 Corinthians 3:5, where does any power and ability we have come from?

   _____

   _____

   _____

   _____

4. Write in your own words what 2 Corinthians 9:8 means.

   _____

   _____

~ Journal ~

Have you ever been faced with a task you felt ill-equipped to do? How does your new understanding of God's enabling power — grace — change your mindset about tackling new things?

_____

_____

_____

_____

_____

_____

_____

_____

_____

_____

_____

_____

_____

_____

_____

_____

_____

_____

_____

Love Ennobles

~≈~

In a great house there are not only vessels of gold and silver, but also [utensils] of wood and earthenware, and some for honorable and noble [use] and some for menial and ignoble [use]. So whoever cleanses himself [from what is ignoble and unclean, who separates himself from contact with contaminating and corrupting influences] will [then himself] be a vessel set apart and useful for honorable and noble purposes, consecrated and profitable to the Master, fit and ready for any good work.

2 Timothy 2:20-21

~≈~

At some point in your relationship with the Lord, you'll graduate from being a spiritual "baby," to being a mature believer. In 1 Corinthians 13:11, Paul says, *"When I was a child, I talked like a child, I thought like a child, I reasoned like a child; now that I have become a man, I am done with childish ways and have put them aside."* One of the attributes of a child is not really being able to differentiate between what is bad and what is good. To a baby, everything is good, at least until it first experiences otherwise. In 2 Timothy 2:20-21, God is telling us to separate ourselves from the influences that could contaminate or corrupt us. This may be something different for each of us. It may be something as simple as not watching a certain television show, or something as complicated as ending a long-standing relationship.

At one point in his life, King David allowed himself

to come under a corrupting influence and have an affair with a beautiful woman, Bathsheba. It eventually led to his murdering her husband. David allowed himself to come under the influence of something that caused harm to many, including himself. But what did he do? Did he brood or wallow in self-pity? No. He went to the Lord, confessed his sin, and turned away from it (repented). God then restored him and his broken relationships.

This is what God asks all believers to do. If at any point in your Christian experience you find yourself not as close to the Lord as you had previously been, it's time to take a personal inventory. In other words, take an inward look at where your heart is in relationship to God. King David, himself, had to do this. In Psalm 139:23-24 he said, *"Search me [thoroughly], O God, and know my heart! Try me and know my thoughts! And see if there is any wicked or hurtful way in me, and lead me in the way everlasting."* David took responsibility for his actions, and went to God to restore their relationship. Because he was faithful to do this, God also restored David's earthly relationships and David is known as the greatest king of Israel.

Second Timothy 2:20-21 tells us we see that if we take responsibility for the things that influence or corrupt our "heart condition," God will be able to trust us. He will then honor us by using us for His noble purposes.

Matthew 20:16 says: *Many are called, but few chosen.* We're all signed up for active duty, but exactly what exciting duty we're called to do is up to us. If you take responsibility for your heart, God will know He can trust you for His noble use. You will be one of His vessels of gold.

~ Life Application ~

1. According to 2 Timothy 2:20-21, what do you have to do to personally prepare yourself for noble use by God? What do you think a vessel of gold and silver is? What is a vessel of wood and earthenware?

   _____

   _____

   _____

   _____

2. Why do you suppose God would use for noble purposes a person who inventories his own heart?

   _____

   _____

   _____

   _____

3. Psalm 51:10 says: *Create in me a clean heart, O God, and renew a right, persevering, and steadfast spirit within me.* What is a clean heart? How do you maintain one?

   _____

   _____

   _____

4. What does Matthew 20:16 mean to you?

   _____

   _____

~ Journal ~

Take a personal inventory of your heart. Is anything standing between you and God? Does your relationship with Him feel vibrant, or stale? Are there any contaminating or corrupting influences in your life? Ask God to search your heart and help you get it right if you need to. How do you feel about your relationship with God now that you've made a clean breast of it?

_____

_____

_____

_____

_____

_____

_____

_____

_____

_____

_____

_____

_____

_____

_____

Love Instructs

~≈~

Through skillful and godly Wisdom is a house (a life, a home, a family) built, and by understanding it is established [on a sound and good foundation], and by knowledge shall its chambers [of every area] be filled with all precious and pleasant riches.

Proverbs 24:3-4

~≈~

All of us want the good life. We want to have a beautiful home, a wonderful loving family, and success in all of our endeavors. This kind of life, however, has eluded some of us because we didn't have a "mentor," someone to instruct us and give us guidance along our journey through life. As a result, we've made a few wrong turns along our way, turns that may have kept us from exactly what we were seeking. Well, never fear! God is here, and His mercies are new every morning. So, forget about the past. Let's start fresh from now.

The Bible is full of instructions, from cover-to-cover, on how to live your life. It has influenced great men and great cultures. God, our heavenly "Mentor" has not left us to fend for ourselves. He has given us His Word as our instruction manual. It is His will, in fact that we live the good life that our hearts desire. Third John 1:2 says: *Beloved, I pray that you may prosper in every way and [that your body] may keep well, even as [I know] your soul keeps well and prospers.* The key to prospering is to have your soul prosper first; then the rest will follow. God's Word inside of you will instruct you and make you prosperous along your life's journey.

Second Timothy 2:15 says this clearly: *Study and be eager and do your utmost to present yourself to God approved (tested by trial), a workman who has no cause to be ashamed, correctly analyzing and accurately dividing [rightly handling and skillfully teaching] the Word of Truth.* God wants you to dive in and study His Word, so that He can teach you how to live. When you do, He'll teach you how to have a prosperous life in every area, and later, you'll be able to teach others.

But, where do you begin? Well, what you're doing right now is a good start. Just continue in the study of God's Word. Make it a lifelong pursuit. John 15:10 says: *If you keep my commandments [if you continue to obey My instructions], you will abide in My love and live on in it, just as I [Jesus] have obeyed My Father's commandments and live on in His love.* The key to continuing in God's love is to learn of Him and to follow His instructions. Then, little by little, you'll find yourself living more and more of the good life, which is not only your heart's desire, but God's will for you from the beginning of time. As Psalm 37:4 says: *Delight yourself also in the Lord, and He will give you the desires and secret petitions of your heart.*

~ Life Application ~

1. Read Proverbs 24:3-4. What does this mean?

   _____

   _____

   _____

   _____

2. According to 2 Timothy 2:15, what kind of workman does God want you to be?

   _____

   _____

   _____

   _____

3. According to 3 John 1:2, in what areas does God want us to prosper?

   _____

   _____

   _____

   _____

4. How does one prosper in spirit? in soul? in body?

   _____

   _____

   _____

   _____

~ Journal ~

Read Proverbs 24:3-4. What do you think are some of the precious and pleasant riches your house will be filled with if you pursue skillful and Godly wisdom?

_____

_____

_____

_____

_____

_____

_____

_____

_____

_____

_____

_____

_____

_____

_____

_____

_____

_____

_____

Love Communicates

~•~

Do not fret or have any anxiety about anything, but in every circumstance and in everything, by prayer and petition (definite requests), with thanksgiving, continue to make your wants known to God.

Philippians 4:6

~•~

Even though God is the Creator of the Universe, too vast for us to understand, He has made a way for us to communicate with Him as we work toward fulfilling His destiny for our lives. This communication is called prayer. At any time during our journey, we can stop and ask God for direction and guidance. Jesus, who never sinned, spent a great deal of time in prayer with God. He even gave us a model prayer: *Our Father Who is in heaven, hallowed (kept holy) be Your name. Your kingdom come, Your will be done on earth as it is in heaven. Give us this day our daily bread. And forgive us our debts, as we also have forgiven (left, remitted, and let go of the debts, and have given up resentment against) our debtors. And lead (bring) us not into temptation, but deliver us from the evil one. For Yours is the kingdom and the power and the glory forever. Amen.* (Matthew 6:9-13)

The Lord's Prayer is our guideline as to how we should pray to God. The first element is worship, where we look toward God, and tell Him how great and awesome He is. This sets the stage and is something He desires of us, and of which He is certainly worthy.

Next, we pray for His kingdom to rule and reign on this earth, first in our hearts, then in others', for His will

— which is best for all of us — to be done.

We then ask Him for our daily bread, which includes both spiritual and material things, like food, clothing, shelter, as well as love, joy, peace, etc. He has promised to provide us with these things, but He wants us to ask Him for them.

We also ask Him to forgive us; but this is contingent on us forgiving others. In this way, things flow smoothly for us in our relationships, and God's will is able to be fulfilled in our own lives as well as others.

We then pray that we will not be led into temptation, and that we will be delivered from the evil one. Satan is always around setting snares for us, but by praying this way, we enlist God's angels on our behalf to protect us and make us aware of our enemy's devices.

Finally, we pray that the kingdom and power and glory are God's, not ours. This helps us keep things in perspective, by giving credit where credit is due, and humbling us so that we don't get "too big for our britches."

All of the above are elements of prayer. There is much more to learn on the subject, but these are the basics. As you incorporate these into your daily prayers, you will find your lines of communication to God more open and free. God desires to communicate with you. As you pray to Him and take time to allow Him to speak to you, you will even begin to hear His "still, small voice" in your heart. No longer will the communication be only a monologue from you to God; it will become a dialogue, as you open your heart more to His will and leading. Use Jesus' example of prayer as a model, and you will find yourself wrapped more and more in God's loving arms. You will then see His kingdom come more abundantly in your own life as well as the lives of those you love.

~ Life Application ~

1. According to Matthew 6:9-13, what are the essential elements of the Lord's prayer? Write them here.

    _____

    _____

    _____

    _____

2. When you pray, why should you request that God's will be done on earth? Why not your will?

    _____

    _____

    _____

3. Why is forgiveness such an important element of prayer?

    _____

    _____

    _____

    _____

4. Why should you pray to be delivered from temptation?

    _____

    _____

    _____

    _____

~ Journal ~

God obviously believes prayer is important. Jesus gave us a perfect example to model our prayers by. How would you describe prayer? What is it for? Why is it necessary? Why does God admonish us not to be anxious, but to pray? Record your thoughts, and then write a brief prayer to God. Include all of the key elements in Matthew 6:9-13.

_____

_____

_____

_____

_____

_____

_____

_____

_____

_____

_____

_____

_____

_____

_____

_____

_____

_____

Love Is Bold

~∾~

Let us then fearlessly and confidently and boldly draw near to the throne of grace (the throne of God's unmerited favor to sinners), that we may receive mercy [for our failures] and find grace to help in good time for every need [appropriate help and well-timed help, coming just when we need it.]

Hebrews 4:16

~∾~

At one time or another, you've probably watched an old-fashioned movie in which the hero saves the heroine from doom just in the nick-of-time. Hebrews 4:16 describes God's help to us in much the same way. When we need help, God wants us to come to Him boldly so He can have mercy on us and save us…just in the nick-of-time. I suppose God likes a little bit of drama just as much as we do, and wants it clearly understood that He's in charge so we can take no credit for His daring rescue.

Trust is the major factor involved in receiving well-timed help from God. We must lean on Him and rely on Him, knowing that our lives are in His hands and that He will take care of us. But rather than being a passive trust, this trust is active. God tells us to go boldly to Him and ask Him for help when we need it. First John 4:18 says *there is no fear in love [dread does not exist], but full-grown (complete, perfect) love turns fear out of doors and expels every trace of terror!* As we draw closer to God, and as we learn more about His love for us, fear loses its grip on us and must go. We can then boldly go to Him when we need something, and He promises to give us appropriate and well-timed help.

Second Timothy 1:7 says that *God did not give us a spirit of timidity (of cowardice, of craven and cringing and fawning fear), but [He has given us a spirit] of power and of love and of calm and well-balanced mind and discipline and self-control.* Many times when we are in dire straits, we're tempted to get anxious and worry about our situation. But God's Word says that timidity and fear are not from Him. He wants us to be bold and come to Him without any reservation. Proverbs 28:1 says: *The wicked flee when no man pursues them, but the [uncompromisingly] righteous are bold as a lion.* Jesus is the "Lion of Judah." We are to be lion-hearted as well. We then, are admonished by God to come to Him boldly when we need help, and He will indeed help us.

What if you need help from God and you don't feel very bold? As you draw near to God, you are drawing near His throne to receive His grace, which, according to James 4:6, is the power of the Holy Spirit, to meet evil tendencies fully. God will help you have courage. He constantly tells us not to fear, because He will never forsake us. Now, you may not feel very bold in a given situation, but if you're bold enough to go to God with your problem, He will provide you with whatever you need to overcome that problem. So, don't feel intimidated the next time you need something from God. Go to Him boldly. He promises to turn your situation around, just in the nick-of-time.

~ Life Application ~

1. According to Hebrews 4:16, how are we supposed to approach God's throne of grace?

   _____

   _____

   _____

   _____

2. What does God promise we can receive from His throne of grace? Is that a good thing?

   _____

   _____

   _____

   _____

3. According to 1 John 4:18, what is the relationship between fear and love? Can they both exist in the same place? Why?

   _____

   _____

   _____

   _____

4. What kind of spirit does 2 Timothy 1:7 say God has given us?

   _____

   _____

   _____

~ Journal ~

God's desire is for us to be "lion-hearted" in approaching Him. What must His heart be toward you if He allows you such access to His throne? Does knowing how He feels about you coming to Him change your opinion of your relationship with Him? Write down your thoughts.

_____

_____

_____

_____

_____

_____

_____

_____

_____

_____

_____

_____

_____

_____

_____

_____

_____

_____

_____

Love Answers

~≈~

Ask and keep on asking and it shall be given you; seek and keep on seeking and you shall find; knock and keep on knocking and the door shall be opened to you. For everyone who asks and keeps on asking receives; and he who seeks and keeps on seeking finds; and to him who knocks and keeps on knocking, the door shall be opened. If you then…know how to give good gifts [gifts that are to their advantage] to your children, how much more will your heavenly Father give the Holy Spirit to those who ask and continue to ask Him!

Luke 11:9-10, 13

~≈~

In the above scripture we see three keys to receiving answers from the Lord: Ask. Seek. Knock. He answers our prayers through His *Holy Spirit, Whom the Father will send in [My] name…He will teach you all things.* (John 14:26.)

Ask. The first key is to ask. A proud, haughty person won't ask for help, but a humble person will. As you study and meditate on God's Word, you'll have questions to ask God; He promises to answer them for you, through His Holy Spirit. No question is foolish. Remain humble when you ask for help, and God's grace will be made available to you.

Seek. The next key is seeking, or searching for, God. Jeremiah 29:13 says: *Then you will seek Me, inquire for, and require Me [as a vital necessity] and find Me when you search for Me with all your heart.* When we esteem God highly, when we treat Him like a great treasure, He promises that we will find Him. Matthew 13:45-46 describes this well: *The kingdom of heaven is like a man who is a dealer in search of fine and precious pearls, who, on finding a single pearl of great price, went and sold all he had and bought it.* Matthew 6:33 tells us: *Seek (aim at and strive after) first of all His kingdom and His righteousness (His way of doing and being right), and then all these things taken together will be given you besides.* God's desire is that we would search for Him and His kingdom with all our might. He promises that through this process of seeking Him and His Word, we will find Him.

Knock. The last key to receiving God's answers is knocking. Here's a good example: *Which of you who has a friend will go to him at midnight and will say to him, "Friend, lend me three loaves [of bread], for a friend of mine who is on a journey has just come, and I have nothing to put before him," and he from within will answer, "Do not disturb me; the door is now closed, and my children are with me in bed; I cannot get up and supply you [with anything]?" I tell you, although he will not get up and supply him anything because he is his friend, yet because of his shameless persistence and insistence he will get up and give him as much as he needs* (Luke 11:5-8). This is an example of the persistent, and insistent faith to which God promises to respond.

So, in your prayer time, continue to ask, seek and knock. This is the kind of faith God likes, persistent and insistent faith that doesn't give up until it gets its answer. Your heavenly Father wants to give you good and advantageous gifts; they're yours, only for the asking.

~ Life Application ~

1. What three things must we do, according to Luke 11:9-10, 13, to receive an answer from God? What part does the Holy Spirit play in all of this?

    _____

    _____

    _____

    _____

2. What does it mean to you to "ask"?

    _____

    _____

    _____

    _____

3. What does it mean to "seek"? According to Jeremiah 29:13, what is God's promise to you if you seek Him?

    _____

    _____

    _____

    _____

4. Why is "knocking" an important element to answered prayer?

    _____

    _____

    _____

    _____

~ Journal ~

God wants us to ask, seek and knock persistently in regard to Him and His Word. His desire is for us to have the kind of faith in Him that doesn't quit. In the future, how will that knowledge affect the way you ask Him for things, seek His kingdom, and knock on His door?

_____

_____

_____

_____

_____

_____

_____

_____

_____

_____

_____

_____

_____

_____

_____

_____

_____

Love Transforms

~∾~

*Walk and live [habitually] in the [Holy] Spirit
[responsive to and controlled and guided by the Spirit];
then you will certainly not gratify the cravings and
desires of the flesh (of human nature without God).*

Galatians 5:16

~∾~

Most of us want our lives to change for the better.
We all have quirks and bad habits that we'd like to get
rid of; in fact some of these behaviors are downright
destructive to our relationships. That's why we make our
list of New Year's resolutions. But more often than not,
they're doomed to failure. Even those of us with the
strongest wills can't seem to keep our resolve to change.

As the third person of the Godhead, the Holy Spirit
is available to you to do a powerful work in your life. He
is God's agent of change in your life. You see, you cannot
truly change yourself…only God can do that. As your
relationship with God grows and deepens, your
personality will start to change as a byproduct of that
relationship. As the Holy Spirit has more access to your
heart, mind, will, and emotions, He will change you from
the inside out. Romans 12:2 tells us: *Do not be conformed
to this world (this age), [fashioned after and adapted to its
external, superficial customs], but be transformed (changed)
by the [entire] renewal of your mind [by its new ideals and*

its new attitude], so that you may prove [for yourselves] what is the good and acceptable and perfect will of God, even the thing which is good and acceptable and perfect [in His sight for you]. While we can change things on the outside, God works on the inside to change both our ideals and attitudes to line up with the wonderful plan He has for our lives.

John 4:24 says: God is a Spirit (a spiritual Being) and those who worship Him must worship Him in spirit and in truth (reality). God wants us to learn about Him and His ways of doing things through His Word, and yield ourselves to His Holy Spirit for change. In fact, Romans 12:1 urges: Make a decisive dedication of your bodies [presenting all your members and faculties] as a living sacrifice, holy (devoted, consecrated) and well pleasing to God, which is your reasonable (rational, intelligent) service and spiritual worship. God actually considers us as worshipping Him when we yield and offer up our personalities for Him to change.

But how do we do this? The answer is simple. Ask Him to change us. Instead of trying to change ourselves when we see something in ourselves we don't like, we ask Him to change us. When we study His Word and see some area of our lives or attitudes which need changing, we yield to Him by asking Him to conform us to His divine plan for us. This is what it means to be humble; not to try to change ourselves, but to let Him change us from within. As we do this, His Holy Spirit will have more access to our lives and will be better able to guide us on our path, as well as transform our personality to be more like Jesus.

~ Life Application ~

1. Read Romans 12:2. What does it say we should do so we aren't conformed to this world?

   _____

   _____

   _____

   _____

2. Who is God's agent of change? According to Galatians 5:16, how do you think the Holy Spirit guides and controls you?

   _____

   _____

   _____

   _____

3. What does renewing your mind have to do with being controlled by the Holy Spirit?

   _____

   _____

   _____

   _____

4. Read Romans 12:1. How do you make your body [all your members and faculties] a living sacrifice to God?

   _____

   _____

   _____

~ Journal ~

Think about areas of your personality, or habits you have, which you would like to change. Write them down. Now, ask the Holy Spirit to help you in these different areas. Keep tabs on your progress over the next several days, weeks, months.

_____

_____

_____

_____

_____

_____

_____

_____

_____

_____

_____

_____

_____

_____

_____

_____

_____

Love Conquers Fear

~∿~

There is no fear in love [dread does not exist], but full-grown (complete, perfect) love turns fear out of doors and expels every trace of terror!

1 John 4:18

~∿~

Many factors motivate our actions, but the worst is probably fear. Too many of us live our lives overly concerned about what the future holds. — Disaster could strike at any moment. I could lose my health, possibly even my life. — These thoughts run through everyone's mind to some extent. Yet, these kinds of thoughts run contrary to the way God wants us to think.

Jesus said, in Matthew 6:25, 27, *"I tell you, stop being perpetually uneasy (anxious and worried) about your life, what you shall eat or what you shall drink; or about your body, what you shall put on. Is not life greater [in quality] than food, and the body [far above and more excellent] than clothing?...And who of you by worrying and being anxious can add one unit of measure (cubit) to his stature or to the span of his life?"*

In these verses, Jesus is telling us that our fears and concerns about the future are unproductive emotions. In verses 28-30, He goes on to say, *"Consider the lilies of the field...they neither toil nor spin. Yet I tell you, even Solomon in all his magnificence (excellence, dignity, and grace) was not arrayed like one of these. But if God so clothes the grass of the field, which today is alive and green and* tomorrow *is tossed into the furnace, will He not much more surely clothe you?"*

God's desire is for us to trust Him to take care of all the aspects of our lives, to put our lives in His control, rather than our own. But just how do we do that?

In Matthew 6:33, Jesus gives us the key: *Seek (aim at and strive after) first of all His kingdom and His righteousness (His way of doing and being right), and then all these things taken together will be given you besides.* This is how we show God that we're trusting Him — by seeking His way of doing things, by doing what He says is right. As we do our part, He promises to do His part, which is taking care of all that we need.

In John 14:23, Jesus says, *"If a person [really] loves Me, he will keep My word [obey My teaching]; and My Father will love him, and We will come to him and make Our home (abode, special dwelling place) with him."* By trusting, obeying, and seeking God, you demonstrate to Him that you love Him. The more you do this, the more you'll come to realize just how much He loves you. His perfect love will come to abide with you and make His home in you; there will be absolutely no place for fear in your life. With God's love in your heart, your only response will be to smile in wondrous anticipation of the future.

～ Life Application ～

1. According to Matthew 6:25-30, who can take the best care of you and, therefore, your future?

   _____

   _____

   _____

   _____

2. Are you to be concerned about your own future? Why?

   _____

   _____

   _____

   _____

3. What common idea runs through John 14:23 and Matthew 6:33?

   _____

   _____

   _____

   _____

4. Why is 1 John 4:18 true?

   _____

   _____

   _____

   _____

~ Journal ~

How can you experience more of God's perfect love? What effect will this have on the way you view your future? Write down some of your concerns about the future. Now give these concerns to God in prayer.

_____

_____

_____

_____

_____

_____

_____

_____

_____

_____

_____

_____

_____

_____

_____

_____

_____

_____

_____

Love Forgives

~∾~

Be merciful (sympathetic, tender, responsive, and compassionate) even as your Father is [all these]…. Acquit and forgive and release (give up resentment, let it drop) and you will be acquitted and forgiven and released.

Luke 6:36-37

~∾~

One of the greatest barriers to having loving relationships, is unforgiveness. We've all been wronged at one time or another by someone; it's an inevitable part of life because we are dealing with imperfect human beings. Our human response is to withdraw, or to cut off or to seek revenge on the offender.

God operates quite differently.

Interestingly enough, God, Who is perfect, and Who has every right to be offended by our actions, has chosen not to hold them against us. First Corinthians 13:5-6, which speaks of God's love says it is not *touchy or fretful or resentful; it takes no account of the evil done to it [it pays no attention to a suffered wrong]. It does not rejoice at injustice and unrighteousness, but rejoices when right and truth prevail.* God, Who is perfect, chooses not to keep account of the evil done to Him. Could it be that He knows something we humans fail to realize?

Unforgiveness, rather than being a single, solitary act, actually creates a cycle. This is what we often fail to realize. When someone offends us, we want them to pay for their actions. But, instead of becoming the victor, in this situation we cause ourselves to become the victim. Our unforgiveness stops the flow of love from our hearts and actually cuts us off from God's love. Matthew 6:14-15 says *if you forgive people their trespasses [their reckless and willful sins, leaving them, letting them go, and giving up resentment], your heavenly Father will also forgive you. But if you do not forgive others their trespasses [their reckless and willful sins, leaving them, letting them go, giving up resentment], neither will your Father forgive you your trespasses.*

Jesus ended the cycle of unforgiveness in your life when He died on the cross for your sins. He paid for not only your sins, but also your neighbor's. Now He has empowered you with the same ability to offer this same forgiveness to others on His behalf. Rather than being something a weak person would do, forgiving others is a sign of strength. It puts you in a position of power. You could wait a million years for someone who's offended you to apologize. It may never happen. God, on the other hand, says that you should go to them and forgive them. You see, God's Kingdom operates from your heart. You can't change another person, but you can choose to forgive. By doing so, you show God that you truly love Him. There's great reward in that. In John 13:34-35 Jesus said, *"I give you a new commandment: that you should love one another. Just as I have loved you, so you too should love one another. By this shall all [men] know that you are My disciples, if you love one another [if you keep on showing love among yourselves]."* By forgiving others, you act like God's child, showing the world that love, righteousness, and truth do prevail. Extend His love to a world badly in need of it. Choose to forgive and be a victor, not a victim.

~ Life Application ~

1. Read Luke 6:36-37. In what way are you to be just like your Heavenly Father?

   _____

   _____

   _____

   _____

2. According to 1 Corinthians 13:5-6, what are some characteristics of God's love?

   _____

   _____

   _____

   _____

3. According to Matthew 6:14-15 can you expect God to forgive you if you don't forgive others?

   _____

   _____

   _____

4. According to John 13:34-35, how will the world know you're a disciple of Jesus?

   _____

   _____

   _____

   _____

~ Journal ~

Think about some of the things God has forgiven you for. Can you think of anyone whom you need to forgive? Ask God to help you if it's difficult. Write your prayer concerning your forgiveness of that person. Over the next several weeks, continue to lift that person in prayer, and watch how God goes to work on your behalf.

_____

_____

_____

_____

_____

_____

_____

_____

_____

_____

_____

_____

_____

_____

_____

_____

_____

Love Restores

~≈~

It was God [personally present] in Christ, reconciling and restoring the world to favor with Himself, not counting up and holding against [men] their trespasses [but cancelling them], and committing to us the message of reconciliation (of the restoration to favor).

2 Corinthians 5:19

~≈~

The above scripture is an example of God's goodness and mercy toward us. If anyone had the right to call us on the carpet for our actions, it would certainly be God. But He's in the restoration business, and because He is love, He keeps no record of the wrongs we've done. In fact, not only does He not require us to pay for our wrongdoings, He wants to restore what we've lost through our own misdeeds. Go figure!

But how can this be? Again, because of the price that Jesus paid for us. He's paid our debt in full. Where sin and suffering have ravaged our lives, God wants to make us whole and better than new! In Isaiah 61:3, God tells us He wants to *grant [consolation and joy] to those who mourn in Zion — to give them an ornament (a garland or diadem) of beauty instead of ashes, the oil of joy instead of mourning, the garment [expressive] of praise instead of a heavy, burdened, and failing spirit — that they may be called oaks of righteousness [lofty, strong, and magnificent, distinguished for uprightness, justice, and right standing with God], the planting of the Lord, that He may be glorified.* God wants to turn our lives around, into something beautiful and lovingly adorned by Him. Then, when people see us, because of what He's done, they'll see what a wonderful God we serve.

Not only does God want to restore and beautify our lives, He wants to use us to restore and beautify the lives of others who have also been ravaged by sin and shame. Isaiah 61:4 says of us: *And they shall rebuild the ancient ruins; they shall raise up the former desolations and renew the ruined cities, the devastations of many generations.* God is so good that He takes us, broken and devastated, unworthy as we are, and turns our lives around so we can help others in the same manner. What does God get out of all this? Isaiah 61:9 tells us: *Their offspring shall be known among the nations and their descendants among the peoples. All who see them [in their prosperity] will recognize and acknowledge that they are the people whom the Lord has blessed.*

God wants to use you to show the world exactly what a good God He is, a God of restoration, and a good and loving Father. What part does He want you to play in all of this? He wants you to believe that He is a God Who's in the restoration business, and to cooperate with His plan. Your job is to draw closer to Him, to resist evil, and to make Him a vital part of your life. He wants you to learn of Him and to pursue Him and His way of doing things. As you do this, you will see God restore not only your life, but also the lives of those you come in contact with as you pursue His kingdom and His righteousness.

~ Life Application ~

1. According to 2 Corinthians 5:19, who has restored the world to favor with God?

   _____

   _____

   _____

   _____

2. In Isaiah 61:3, what does God promise to do for you?

   _____

   _____

   _____

   _____

3. What does Isaiah 61:4 mean? Can you see yourself doing that?

   _____

   _____

   _____

   _____

4. According to Isaiah 61:9, what is God's purpose in restoring your life?

   _____

   _____

   _____

   _____

~ Journal ~

God has a wonderful plan for your life as well as the lives of others. Imagine what your life will be like when God fully restores it to you. What will you be able to do for yourself, for your family, for others?

_____

_____

_____

_____

_____

_____

_____

_____

_____

_____

_____

_____

_____

_____

_____

_____

Love Completes

~≈~

He Who began a good work in you will continue until the day of Jesus Christ [right up to the time of His return], developing [that good work] and perfecting and bringing it to full completion in you.

Philippians 1:6

~≈~

God's love not only starts a good work in us, it finishes it. He won't leave us to fend for ourselves. He will actually be there, every step of the way, helping us become what He intends for us to be. As we fellowship with God, we'll become more and more like Him. Colossians 2:7-10 admonishes us: *Have the roots [of your being] firmly and deeply planted [in Him, fixed and founded in Him], being continually built up in Him, becoming increasingly more confirmed and established in the faith…For in Him the whole fullness of Deity [the Godhead] continues to dwell in bodily form [giving complete expression of the divine nature]. And you are in Him, made full and having come to fullness of life [in Christ you too are filled with the Godhead — Father, Son and Holy Spirit — and reach full spiritual stature.]*

God's divine nature in us helps us mature as believers as we give it access to every part of ourselves; heart, soul, mind and strength. We are then motivated by the very same things that God is, and can therefore serve Him more fully. We can thus fulfill Ephesians 4:1, which tells us to *walk (lead a life) worthy of the [divine] calling to which you have been called*

[with behavior that is a credit to the summons to God's service.]

Many of us think it's our job to perfect ourselves, so every setback we encounter discourages us from continuing our journey. The truth is, God began the good work in us by calling us to a divine destiny, and He is the One Who will finish the job. It takes an awfully big load off of our shoulders. That's why Jesus says in Matthew 11:28-30, *"Come to Me, all you who labor and are heavy-laden and overburdened, and I will cause you to rest. [I will ease and relieve and refresh your souls.] Take My yoke upon you and learn of Me, for I am gentle (meek) and humble (lowly) in heart, and you will find rest (relief and ease and refreshment and recreation and blessed quiet) for your souls. For My yoke is wholesome (useful, good — not harsh, hard, sharp, or pressing, but comfortable, gracious, and pleasant), and My burden is light and easy to be borne."*

God has a plan for your life, but He is the One Who will complete the work in you. Your part is this: to remain meek, which means to be open for God to teach you; and to remain humble, which means you must have a proper understanding of your relationship with God, not thinking either too highly or too lowly of yourself. God says if you do your part, He will refresh you on your journey, and the "burden" you bear will be light (which means comfortable, gracious, pleasant, and easy to be borne). Don't try to perfect yourself. Let God, the only "perfect" One, do the perfecting in you. Remember, you're in His expert hands, and He knows how to get the job done.

~ Life Application ~

1. What does Philippians 1:6 mean to you?

   _____

   _____

   _____

   _____

2. What does it mean that God perfects and completes you?

   _____

   _____

   _____

   _____

3. Read Colossians 2:7, 9-10. What do you think it means to reach full spiritual stature?

   _____

   _____

   _____

   _____

4. Read Matthew 11:28-30 again. Why does knowing Who completes you make your burden light?

   _____

   _____

   _____

   _____

～Journal～

Now that you've learned that God will perfect and complete you, does it help you view your future differently than you had in the past? Are you relieved?

_____

_____

_____

_____

_____

_____

_____

_____

_____

_____

_____

_____

_____

_____

_____

_____

_____

Love Rewards

~~∾~~

*Blessed (happy, to be envied) is the man who is patient
under trial and stands up under temptation, for when
he has stood the test and been approved, he will receive
[the victor's] crown of life which God has promised to
those who love Him.*

James 1:12

~~∾~~

Doing things God's way and operating in the principles
of His kingdom is a noble pursuit with many benefits and
rewards. Psalm 19:7-11 says, *"The law of the Lord is perfect,
restoring the [whole] person; the testimony of the Lord is sure,
making wise the simple. The precepts of the Lord are right,
rejoicing the heart; the commandment of the Lord is pure and
bright, enlightening the eyes. The [reverent] fear of the Lord is
clean, enduring forever; the ordinances of the Lord are true and
righteous altogether. More to be desired are they than gold, even
than much fine gold; they are sweeter also than honey and
drippings from the honeycomb. Morever, by them is Your servant
warned (reminded, illuminated, and instructed); and in keeping
them there is great reward."* David is telling us that keeping
God's Word will bring us great reward.

At times in our spiritual walk, however, especially
when we are pressing into a new level of understanding
God and His ways, we will be faced with various
temptations and trials — from not wanting to go the extra
mile and believe God for something, to an outright assault
by the enemy. At these times we may not want to speak
and act in agreement with God's Word. King David,
himself, suffered much opposition from his own people
and family, even though God had chosen him to become

king of Israel. Just because God has a plan for your life, don't think it's going to be easy every step of the way. At times you'll encounter resistance; many times it will be from those you think should know better. King David's own brothers didn't think He could defeat Goliath. But David knew God and His Word, so despite opposition, he chose to take God at His Word. He didn't allow opposition to keep him from defeating Goliath and receiving his full reward (King Saul's daughter and, ultimately, rule of Israel).

You too, will have occasions when you'll be tempted to back away from God on your journey. But there's an encouraging word from Jesus in John 16:33: *"In Me you may have [perfect] peace and confidence. In the world you have tribulation and trials and distress and frustration; but be of good cheer [take courage; be confident, certain, undaunted]! For I have overcome the world. [I have deprived it of power to harm you and have conquered it for you.]"* Jesus' death and resurrection made it possible for you to have victory over any opposition that comes your way. If you hold fast to your faith and confess it, you will receive your reward.

No matter what battle you face in life, whether financial, health, or the deliverance of a loved one, don't allow an attack of any kind to stop you from obtaining your reward. God has a good plan for not only your life, but also the lives of those you love. He has a great reward for you. Keep on keeping on until you receive your full benefits.

Isaiah 54:17 says: *No weapon that is formed against you shall prosper, and every tongue that shall rise against you in judgment you shall show to be in the wrong. This [peace, righteousness, security, triumph over opposition] is the heritage of the servants of the Lord.* Keep this in mind as you move along on your spiritual journey. God's love will get you through every time, and at the end of every journey, you'll receive your reward.

~ Life Application ~

1. What do you have to do, according to James 1:12, to receive the victor's crown?

   _____

   _____

   _____

   _____

2. Read Psalm 19:7-11. What are some of the rewards it speaks of?

   _____

   _____

   _____

   _____

3. Read John 16:33. What comfort does Jesus give you concerning tribulation, trials and distress?

   _____

   _____

   _____

   _____

4. According to Isaiah 54:17, what is the heritage of the servants of the Lord?

   _____

   _____

   _____

~ Journal ~

Have you been tempted to back away from God's Word in some area? What kind of opposition were you facing at that time? If you were to face a similar situation now, in light of what you've just read, how might you handle it differently? Do you believe you can receive the victor's crown in that situation? Write down your thoughts.

_____

_____

_____

_____

_____

_____

_____

_____

_____

_____

_____

_____

_____

_____

_____

_____

Love Strengthens

~∾~

Be not grieved and depressed, for the joy of the Lord is your strength and stronghold.

Nehemiah 8:10

~∾~

Attitude is everything. Many of us exercise and take vitamin supplements so that we'll stay strong enough to fend off physical ailments. It helps us keep our attitudes good so we feel strong enough to face the future.

But our spirits can also come under attack; and God has an antidote — joy. With it He doesn't just strengthen our bodies, He strengthens our hearts, souls and minds as well.

While many of us concentrate on the superficial aspects of health, God works from the inside out. You can have the strongest body in the world, but if you're damaged mentally and emotionally, your life won't be the success it could be.

That's why God's antidote for weakness or a bad attitude is joy. As you come to know more and more about your loving heavenly Father, the promises He has given you in His Word will be something you can hold on to. The more you understand how strong and powerful and great He is, the "bigger" He will grow in your eyes. This is "magnifying God." Now, when you magnify God, you're actually praising Him — telling Him how wonderful He is. As you do this, you'll find yourself having more and more access to God's person and His power. And it's not a hard thing to do, but easy and joyful. As you magnify and praise the Lord, your heart will fill with overflowing love for God and others.

In Psalm 100, David says, *"Make a joyful noise to the Lord all you lands! Serve the Lord with gladness! Come before His presence with singing! Know (perceive, recognize and understand with approval) that the Lord is God! It is He Who has made us, not we ourselves [and we are His]! We are His people and the sheep of His pasture. Enter into His gates with thanksgiving and a thank offering and into His courts with praise! Be thankful and say so to Him, bless and affectionately praise His name! For the Lord is good; His mercy and loving-kindness are everlasting, His faithfulness and truth endure to all generations."*

Having a joyful attitude is an important part of making ourselves available to God's plan for us. It opens us up to what God has in store for us; it helps us focus on the possibilities, not the impossibilities. Proverbs 4:23 says: *Keep and guard your heart with all vigilance and above all that you guard, for out of it flow the springs of life.* Joy is a sign that all is well in our relationship with God, and that our hearts are overflowing with His love. We can be full of joy and thanksgiving to God because we have total confidence that He will take care of us. So make a joyful noise to God, praising, magnifying and thanking Him — and watch your spiritual muscles grow!

~ Life Application ~

1. What's the antidote for grief and depression?

   _____

   _____

   _____

   _____

2. Read Psalm 100 again. How did he tell us to enter God's gates and courts? Why is thanksgiving so important?

   _____

   _____

   _____

   _____

3. What was David's attitude toward God? Did he have joy?

   _____

   _____

   _____

   _____

4. According to Proverb 4:23, where does joy come from? Why should you guard your heart?

   _____

   _____

   _____

   _____

~ Journal ~

Now that you know the joy of the Lord is your strength and stronghold, what are some things you can do to maintain more joy in your life?

_____

_____

_____

_____

_____

_____

_____

_____

_____

_____

_____

_____

_____

_____

_____

_____

_____

_____

_____

Love Is Eternal

~≈~

For now we are looking in a mirror that gives only a dim (blurred) reflection [of reality as in a riddle or enigma], but then [when perfection comes] we shall see in reality and face to face! Now I know in part (imperfectly), but then I shall know and understand fully and clearly, even in the same manner as I have been fully and clearly known and understood [by God]. And so faith, hope, love abide [faith — conviction and belief respecting man's relation to God and divine things; hope — joyful and confident expectation of eternal salvation; love — true affection for God and man, growing out of God's love for and in us], these three; but the greatest of these is love.

1 Corinthians 13:12-13

~≈~

A relationship with God, and understanding the full impact of His love for us are things we will need an eternity to pursue. God considers this pursuit the most important thing we can do with our lives. In truth, He set the whole universe in motion for the purpose of demonstrating to us just how very much we are loved. But many of us find this concept difficult to understand. How could so great a God be concerned with us, mere human beings? It seems unfathomable. In Psalm 8:1, 3-6, David echoes these very thoughts: *"O Lord, our Lord, how excellent (majestic and glorious) is Your name in all the earth! You have set Your glory on [or above] the heavens….When I view and consider Your heavens, the work of Your fingers, the moon and the stars, which You have ordained and established, What is man that You are mindful of him, and the son of [earthborn] man that You care for him? Yet You have made him but a little lower than God [or heavenly beings], and You have crowned him with glory and honor. You made him to have dominion over the works of Your hands; You have put all things under his feet."* The awesomeness of God's love for us cannot be expressed any better than David expresses it here.

God loves you so much that He has set in motion a marvelous plan, tailor-made just for you. Not only that, He has made available to you everything you need for that plan to succeed. The question is, will you open yourself up to Him — by trusting Him, by learning of Him, by agreeing with His Word despite circumstances — so that He can help you fulfill your specific purpose as part of His great design?

God desires your love. This is the sum total of what you were created for, to be in eternal fellowship with Him. As you are, He promises to bless your life abundantly as well as your relationships with others. Will you answer His call to love Him with all your heart, soul, mind and strength? Will you make love your chief aim in life? If you do so, He promises that you won't be disappointed because love's got everything to do with it. It never fails.

~ Life Application ~

1. According to 1 Corinthians 13:12-13, of faith, hope and love, why is love considered the greatest?

    _____

    _____

    _____

    _____

2. How is love described in this scripture?

    _____

    _____

    _____

    _____

3. According to the definition, will understanding God's love for you and in you help you love others better? Why?

    _____

    _____

    _____

    _____

4. First Corinthians 13:8 says: *Love never fails [never fades out or becomes obsolete or comes to an end]*. How does this comfort you?

    _____

    _____

    _____

~ Journal ~

How has your view of love changed from when you began this book? What aspects of God's love have really made the deepest impression on you? Have your ideas about love changed? How have you changed?

_____

_____

_____

_____

_____

_____

_____

_____

_____

_____

_____

_____

_____

_____

_____

_____

_____

_____

Answers to Prayer

Date Made	Prayer Request	Date Received
_____	_____	_____
_____	_____	_____
_____	_____	_____
_____	_____	_____
_____	_____	_____
_____	_____	_____
_____	_____	_____
_____	_____	_____
_____	_____	_____
_____	_____	_____
_____	_____	_____
_____	_____	_____
_____	_____	_____
_____	_____	_____
_____	_____	_____
_____	_____	_____
_____	_____	_____
_____	_____	_____
_____	_____	_____
_____	_____	_____
_____	_____	_____
_____	_____	_____
_____	_____	_____
_____	_____	_____

Answers to Prayer

Date Made	Prayer Request	Date Received
_____	_____	_____
_____	_____	_____
_____	_____	_____
_____	_____	_____
_____	_____	_____
_____	_____	_____
_____	_____	_____
_____	_____	_____
_____	_____	_____
_____	_____	_____
_____	_____	_____
_____	_____	_____
_____	_____	_____
_____	_____	_____
_____	_____	_____
_____	_____	_____
_____	_____	_____
_____	_____	_____
_____	_____	_____
_____	_____	_____
_____	_____	_____
_____	_____	_____
_____	_____	_____
_____	_____	_____

Answers to Prayer

Date Made	Prayer Request	Date Received
_____	_____	_____
_____	_____	_____
_____	_____	_____
_____	_____	_____
_____	_____	_____
_____	_____	_____
_____	_____	_____
_____	_____	_____
_____	_____	_____
_____	_____	_____
_____	_____	_____
_____	_____	_____
_____	_____	_____
_____	_____	_____
_____	_____	_____
_____	_____	_____
_____	_____	_____
_____	_____	_____
_____	_____	_____
_____	_____	_____
_____	_____	_____
_____	_____	_____
_____	_____	_____

Notes

Notes

Notes

Notes

Notes

Notes